DRIVERS

Creating Trust and Motivation at Work

Susanne Jacobs

DRIVERS

First published in 2017 by

Panoma Press Ltd
48 St Vincent Drive, St Albans, Herts, AL1 5SJ, UK
info@panomapress.com
www.panomapress.com

Book layout by Neil Coe.

Printed on acid-free paper from managed forests.

ISBN 978-1-784521-18-9

For my husband Tim, without whose enduring support this book would never have been written. And for Emma and Annabel who are my reason why.

TESTIMONIALS

Leaders who make a difference rather than just make the numbers are hard to find. There has never been a better time to share the insight and wisdom within this book. The DRIVERS model is a highly practical way to engage people in meaningful dialogue about what brings us to work, what keeps us there and what enables us to contribute in extraordinary ways. It works because it adopts a deeply human and therefore deeply meaningful strategy to create the conditions for people to thrive in ways they never imagined.

Dr Carole Edmond
Founder of glassmoon and Managing Director, The Regard Group

We talk about the Future of Work, but in fact the Fourth Industrial Revolution is here and any enlightened company should be proofing for how this will impact their people. At the heart of the employee lifecycle is the need to trust your people and for them to trust you. We are now successfully using Susanne's DRIVERS model to influence our leaders' mindsets to empower their people, giving them a voice and a choice to develop that trust and nurture it through behaviour changes that deliver value for everyone.

Fleur Bothwick OBE
Director of Diversity & Inclusive Leadership, EY

CONTENTS

INTRODUCTION

Over a decade ago I set out to understand what really motivates us. To learn and apply the science of and for optimal performance. Why? Well, I'd spent over 20 years in the corporate environment with the latter ten years of my time in senior leadership. My roles have been mainly focused on transformation, which comes in many guises but all mean change. I managed many large projects, often the corporate equivalent of the hokey-cokey – insource, outsource, shake it all about! I witnessed these change programmes being done well in pockets but most failed to achieve their original objectives and caused anguish to all those involved. I worked with teams who seem to be naturally engaged and willing, and as the saying goes 'to go the extra mile'. And I experienced teams where energy and motivation seem a distant past, where relationships crack, gossip and sabotage invade and individuals fall foul of distress and become ill.

My role as a leader, in my eyes, has always been to support every individual to thrive – to build teams where everyone wants to be, but I didn't have the instruction manual. I led well but I felt blind. I wanted to understand the wiring of the humans I led, to know how to really motivate them rather than floundering with well-intended but not always successful team-building events or additional benefits. I grew tired of the annual engagement survey that only took a snapshot of an individual's work-life and which could have been completed on a sunny Friday afternoon or a rainy Monday morning giving very different viewpoints. Whatever my engagement scores on the doors, the ensuing reports didn't tell me the 'what' or the 'how' and left me with more questions than answers.

What really motivates us? What is the human science of engagement? How could I lead to both enhance wellbeing and sustain performance?

I wanted to know the answers to these questions, so over a decade ago I set out to find them. This book is the result of my research and my experience with a spoonful or two of my opinion. I want to share what I have learned with you about how we can create better workplace environments where we can thrive, engage, and give and be of our best because we want to, not because the carrots or the sticks tell us to.

Enjoy.

Susanne

CHAPTER 1
DRIVERS

'Trust is the glue of life. It's the most essential ingredient in effective communication.

It's the foundational principle that holds all relationships.'

Stephen Covey

Trust – the true performance currency

Today I boarded the train to work and trusted that the driver would get me to my destination in one piece and that every passenger meant me no harm. These thoughts were not conscious, it just was. I got to work and walked through the grand revolving doors into a place where, unlike the world outside, I know many people but do not really trust anyone.

We use trust every day to make our way through the world – whether it's walking down the street, driving on the motorway, or simply crossing the road. We place our trust in others who, more often than not, we will never actually meet. Trust as a term is used frequently within the corporate world. There is a desire to build it, get it, secure it, but I am yet to come across a leader who really understands how to do this or even what trust is. Trust sits as an ethereal concept rather than a tangible action. Putting 'grow trust' on the list of expected leadership behaviours or within the business values does not give the instructions on the how or the what or even the why. Akin to telling someone to eat healthily or to get fit, the instruction doesn't work because we don't have the knowledge to even start.

Paul Zak's work in neuroeconomics discovered that trust is among the strongest known predictors of a country's wealth; nations with low levels tend to be poor.[1] The neuropeptide oxytocin is released in direct correlation to the level of trust. As oxytocin rises, so does the perceived trustworthiness of an individual. Oxytocin calms the fear centres of your brain and boosts serotonin release, the feel-good neurochemical. It is literally rewarding to trust and be trusted.

Distrust, on the other hand, plays out in offices all over the world through behaviours such as gossiping, micro-management and battles for maintaining individual power. The damage is to our emotional engagement, creativity and ultimately our performance and wellbeing. Distrust leads to distress, which hinders the production of oxytocin. Relationships start to falter slowing down every interaction as suspicion creeps in. As Stephen Covey puts it: '*Financial success comes from success in the marketplace, and success in the marketplace comes from success in the workplace. The heart and soul of all of this is trust.*'[2]

Our brain's primary function is to keep us out of harm's way by ensuring that we are always motivated to go towards safety and away from threat – a simple premise controlled by the most complex system in our known universe. Trust is neurological safety. When we move towards safety we are neurochemically rewarded – intrinsically motivating us to do more of what keeps us alive and flourishing by flooding our physiology with health-protecting hormones delivering feel-good sensations. So, think about it, this process is fundamental to why we do what we do. What if we can create workplaces that support and leverage this natural biological reward mechanism? And, if so, what are the factors that our brain equates as trust?

The answer is the DRIVERS – a trust checklist drawn from various fields of science including evolutionary biology, cognitive neuroscience, psychology and anthropology. The DRIVERS establish and embed trust sparking intrinsic motivation and reward. I have written this book to share the DRIVERS with you. To evidence for you why each of the DRIVERS is fundamental for trust and how, if each are supported in the workplace, intrinsic motivation, engagement, improved wellbeing and sustainable performance are the results.

So here goes…

The DRIVERS

D	Direction	A clear sense of purpose and meaning
R	Relative position	My sense of significance, identity and position within my group, that my contribution is understood and valued by others
I	Inclusion	My perception of belonging
V	Voice and Choice	My sense that my view will be heard and that I have choice, autonomy and control over my decisions that affect my life
E	Equity	My perception of being treated fairly and of fairness and equity within my group
R	Reliability	My sense of certainty and security in my surroundings, others and my life
S	Stretch	My opportunities for growth, learning and achievement through effort

Each of the DRIVERS has an evolutionary and survival benefit and my research shows their correlation to trust.[3] When the brain perceives each of the DRIVERS to be supported we not only feel safe but we also get that all important feel-good chemical reward, the seat of intrinsic motivation.

Trust – the performance currency

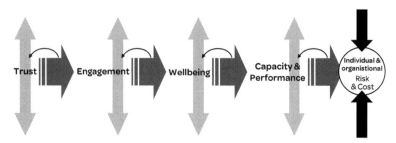

Each of the DRIVERS is correlated to each other. In other words, support one you will support the others, but quash one you will quash them all, leaving them to fall like skittles. This is vital to understand as it can work for and against leadership. For example, change is a threat for the brain – I'll explain why later in the book. Change derails reliability and left unchecked the other DRIVERS will start to crack intensifying the level of threat. We can, however, focus on building up the other DRIVERS to ease and offset the impact. Ensuring, for example, that individuals know that their views are heard and that they really feel they belong to the team will help to mitigate the natural threat reaction caused by diminished reliability and certainty.

Don't just take my word for it though. Whilst I have carried out primary research to test the DRIVERS, I have also spent several years exploring academic research and evidence from across many scientific fields of study. My work has been focused on pulling together all the elements of trust and intrinsic motivation into one place so it can be translated and practically applied to the workplace. After all, research is crucial but if it remains only as a paper sat on the proverbial shelf, the value is lost. The true value of knowledge is in its application.

Who are we really?

Before we start to explore the DRIVERS, we need to first understand how our perception shifts our brain's view of whether the DRIVERS are being supported or quashed. To do this we first need to explore how we interpret our world and why we can have very differing views of what is happening to the DRIVERS, even in the same situation.

I have fond memories of walking to school every day with my friend pondering the world as you do at the ripe old age of ten. We talked about everything from what we would do if we were prime minister (free ice cream of course) to what is the point of flies. One such conversation that has stuck with me was, 'Who and what really makes us, us?' I recall saying to my friend as we dawdled across the field that we aren't our arms or our legs – after all, cut these off, things change but we are still us. And, how did we know that what we each saw was the same? Just because you know that a colour is red, is it the same red that I see? Even then I knew 'us' and the meaning we make of the world was what was inside our heads. What I couldn't fathom was how something as clear as me was yet so intangible. Many years of life and exploration since has given me some of the insight into our own unique reality.

Our brain is the most eloquent of all storytellers and the narrative it feeds us gives us… us. This 3lb organ of jelly-like substance, about 2% of our body mass, remains the most complex object known to man. It demands around 20% of our resting metabolic rate, consuming for the typical adult around 260 calories – about the same as a high-intensity aerobic session (I've always thought it a shame that we can't simply think ourselves into better shape!). It has 100 billion cells with several hundred trillion connections using electrochemical signals to create the most intricate network in the world. The brain is continually demanding its main energy source, glucose, to function (before it is converted to adenosine triphosphate (ATP), the main energy currency across the brain cells). Although when compared to man-made computer systems, it is incredibly efficient. The IBM super computer requires 90 IBM powered 750 servers each requiring 1000 watts whereas our brain just needs 20 watts.

When we are born, in comparison to other animals we are helpless. At birth, our brains are not fully formed. We need to establish attachment with a caregiver for survival, without which our brain's growth will be stunted, something I explore within the chapter on Inclusion. It is our environment and our experiences that wire up our brain's circuitry adapting the connections as we go according to the surroundings we are born or move into. You have never existed before and you will never exist again. Your brain wiring is as unique to you as your fingerprints. Our story is ours alone.

The advantage of this unfinished state as we emerge into the world is our ability to adapt to our environment, whether that is the deserts of Egypt or the volcanic landscape of Iceland. From birth to around the age of two our brains make the greatest number of connections, around two million a second, as we soak up the information from the space around us. As we reach two we have around twice as many neural connections as we will have as an adult – but here's the magic. The 'us' of us begins to emerge through the connections we then lose and those that we strengthen. As we focus on learning relevant skills for our surroundings, we start to specialise our neural connections building efficient neural highways that allow us to mould and fit to our world.

This neural building is a risky strategy as our outside world does not always provide what we need but the survival and evolutionary advantage outweighs the threat – the opportunity cost of adaptation. As we grow, our genetic pattern takes our brains on a programmed developmental journey that affects our thoughts and behaviour through teens and on into our adulthood. Most of the greatest changes in our brains are completed by our early twenties, which is almost a quarter of the way through our life. The brain remains, however, capable of change – a property known as neuroplasticity. This plasticity, derived from the Greek to mould or sculpt, allows us to continually adapt the structural makeup of our brain to meet environmental and societal shifts and to learn new skills. As we lay down new neural connections, strengthening them with practice and exposure we are continually building 'us'.

Our story

Who we are changes as we travel through our life. Our interpretation of the world, our reality, is constructed from our past experiences stored in our memory. Our memory, the processing for which is closely related to several organs deep within our brain in an area known as the limbic system, is the filing cabinet of our learning and experience built from all the data we have taken in since we arrived on the earth. Our narrative is built from everything from our culture, religion and schooling to our parents and life events. The files hold our story and our beliefs and rules about the world. Every time we recall an event we are reconstructing data from the filing cabinet's neural connections associated with the past. Memory is not videotape. It is not reliable, using shortcuts and heuristics to build our reality. Its reconstruction is not designed to provide an accurate detailed description of exactly what happened. Instead its role is to hold the indexed files in readiness to rapidly interpret the world and triage the data for threat. Information via our senses is processed through our filing cabinet to first match the data against past experience, categorise its gradient of safety or threat, to then predict what will happen next and finally instruct our physical self on the best course of action. And all of this happens extremely fast without your conscious awareness. The filing cabinet is running the show. If an event is matched as danger then the threat circuitry is triggered – a micro-second reaction within our physiology that redistributes energy and blood flow away from non-essential processes such as our digestion and cognition to parts of our bodies such as the heart and muscles, to prepare us to defend or escape – fight or flight. If, however, the event is deemed safe then this interpretive process may be to simply acknowledge, ignore and allow us to continue on our way, blissfully unaware of what has taken place within our brain.

Our neurology is ancient, trying to keep us alive in a world very different from its origin. We only came off the Savannah some 60,000 to 80,000 years ago, a blink in the evolutionary eye. Most of our threats today are psychological not physical: the looming deadline, a difficult customer or that presentation. The neurochemical response is, however, the same as facing the sabre-toothed tiger. Whilst a vital survival mechanism and great for short-term concentration, over time, left unchecked it causes havoc to our cognitive performance, decision making and relationships, not to mention the neurochemical impact on our health. So many of our workplaces are running on threat. Gallup's 30-year study on employee engagement, detailed in their 'State of the Global Workforce' report, shows that most employees are disengaged. Perhaps their study should be retitled as the 'State of Global Workforce Threat'. We have unintentionally created workplaces that are set up in opposition to our biology. What is this storing up for our health and economy?

The filing and ordering of experience is made possible by our emotions – the librarian. As specifics of events fade we are left with only categorised associations, ready and waiting to respond to the call to match and interpret events. We use our files to recall the past, make sense of the present and run simulations of an imagined future. I am the interconnection of my neurons, my private experience of being me as I make my own personal meaning about my world.

At some point in my life I learned what a chair is and that, on its own, it poses no threat, filed under benign. But since my sister's car accident the sound of a siren sends shivers down my spine urging my body to escape. The reason I can choose not to run is a capability that evolved after our limbic system. Our neo-cortex, the newest part of our brain, provides us, amongst other things, with rational thought and the power of veto over our primary emotional response. Our ability to become more aware of the filing cabinet's interpretation (our perception), regulate the emotions and then use our rational self to choose another course of action to the one instructed by our limbic system is the foundation of resilience. Because of neuroplasticity, resilience can be learnt. Resilient individuals have up to 30 times more activity in their frontal lobes and more neural connections between the upper and lower regions of the brain. This means that whilst they will still feel the impact of the filing cabinet's primary emotional response to events, the strengthened communication channels from their upper brain's rational cortex increases their capacity for dampening the effect, to check and reappraise the first interpretation, and to move to find solutions to challenging situations faster.

This book is not about building resilience, although there are evidenced cognitive tools and techniques to do so in which I strongly believe. The key message here is that our perception is the starting point. It drives our neurochemistry. Perception is affected by our levels of resilience, mood state, psychological and physical health, priming from the environment, fatigue and hunger levels, which all affects the interpretation and prediction process of the data through our filing cabinet. Our perception about what is happening to the DRIVERS for us at any given moment can shift, determining whether our brain interprets them to be safe or under threat. This interpretation is designed to drive our behaviour towards safety and away from danger. It is the basis of whether we engage or disengage.

As leaders, we need to first hear the individual's perception of the DRIVERS to establish what is happening for them. We may not always be able to relate to their view, but ultimately if they believe that any one of the DRIVERS is being quashed their brain will have kick-started the threat response and, no matter what happens next, if this is not put right then performance will suffer.

'Seek first to understand, then be understood.'
Stephen Covey

DIRECTION, PURPOSE AND MEANING

'He who has a why to live can bear almost any how.'

Friedrich Nietzche

The What...

So today you get up at the normal time, follow the normal routine, leave the house at the normal time and take the car/train/bus to work where you arrive at your allotted time. You offer the usual greetings to colleagues as you hang up your coat and go to grab the first coffee/tea of the day. Then to work. A bit of task ordering and shuffling before getting started. Today there'll be nothing out of the ordinary or that you haven't done before. The workload grows as budgets shrink, targets expand and initiatives circle like birds of prey. A full day is always longer than the contracted 9 till 5, which is broken only by the brief relief of a snatched lunch and too many procrastinating coffee breaks. And, although it's been non-stop, you still don't feel as if everything is completed or that there have been any specific achievements made. There's the end of the day, the usual farewells, and the same journey home with the other indistinctive commuters jostling for personal space. And tomorrow... well, the same again. It's not a bad existence but I'd argue it's an empty one – at least in terms of work. To fill the void that so many employees feel in their day-to-day working worlds takes a sense of purpose, direction and meaning, all of which must fit with the employee's own values. This means instilling a sense that what is done in work is worthwhile, intrinsically valuable and has a point. As American author, historian and Pulitzer Prize winner Louis 'Studs' Terkel said, 'Work is about the search for daily meaning as well as daily bread.'

In Greek mythology, Sisyphus was punished by the gods for his dishonesty. He was condemned to push a boulder constantly uphill only for it to roll back down again once he reached the top. Prisoners in the Haidari concentration camp in WWII were put to labour in two four-hour shifts, but the labour was not intended to have a productive result. Instead it was designed to break the prisoners' morale, making them dig holes only to fill them in again, and build walls only to then break them down. With no goal, no reason, no purpose, this futile work is often referred to in behavioural economics as the Sisyphic condition.[4] We are not automatons. We need to care about why and for what purpose we do the things that we do, which in behavioural economics is termed as the Meaningful Condition.[5]

Dan Ariely carried out an experiment to look at the need for meaning from our labour. He asked participants if they would like to build a Lego bionicle (a small Lego model) for $3. When they said yes and completed the bionicle the researchers took it and put it under the table, after which they asked the participants if they'd like to build another for $2.70. After they said yes, they put this one under the table and asked if they'd like to build one more for $2.40, then $2.10 and so on until individuals said it wasn't worth it anymore and stopped. This experiment had been explained to them. They had been told before they started that once everything was finished the bionicles would be disassembled and then used again for the next participant. This established a meaningful condition – a reason for their effort and contribution. The second experiment then followed the same pattern but at each point, as the participant started to build the next bionicle, the previous bionicle was taken apart in front of them, leading to an endless cycle of building and destroying – the Sisyphic condition. The result? Well, in the meaningful condition experiment significantly more bionicles were built (11 versus 7 respectively). And not only that, Ariely also found that those participants who had a greater love for Lego did unsurprisingly build more bionicles within the meaningful condition experiment, but in the Sisyphic experiment this correlation was zero.

He suggests that the lack of purpose by breaking their work up in front of them eliminated any intrinsic reward. I appreciate these are Lego models and this is an experiment, but Ariely's work translates directly to the workplace and the depletion of motivation in the face of meaningless activity. Imagine for a moment your manager asks you to carry out some research about the feasibility of a new project.

You accept and for the next couple of days work on pulling together the risks, returns, investment, stakeholders and so on. You print off the report, walk up to your manager's door and knock. You enter, smile, and hand him the report and start to explain your approach. He puts up his hand, takes the report and puts in on the recycling pile, telling you that they had abandoned the idea of the project. How do you feel? Now replay this scenario, but this time your manager takes your report, says thank you for all the effort you had taken, that unfortunately it looks like the project won't go ahead after all but that he will read your findings as your work will be a great source of learning. How do you feel now? The project is not happening in either scene but the second provides meaning whereas the first sets up Sisyphus's futility of effort. The second delivers intrinsic reward, the first demotivation.

Purpose in practice

A life with purpose is one with direction and a sense of meaning. It gives us a reason for getting up in the morning, for striving to reach a goal and work for an output that supports a value close to our hearts. It drives us to leave a legacy, something by which we will be remembered even when we are no longer around to care. Without purpose there is futility, a sense that what is being done is pointless. This is no different for our working lives. To go to work every day feeling connected and contributing to a clear purpose and direction is hugely motivating. To spend our days in repetitive cycles or with no sense of meaning is demotivating. To be able to answer the 'why I do' in relation to the 'what I do' gives us, and those we speak to, a clarity around the reason for our roles rather than just the 'it pays the bills' rationale.

Rosabeth Moss Kanter, a professor at Harvard Business School, studied motivation in the workplace. She identified meaning as a key motivator. She looked at why the happiest people tackle and dedicate much of their lives to some of the most challenging and difficult problems: turning around inner-city schools, working to feed the homeless or caring for terminally ill children without a penny in return. She says, *'People can be inspired if they care about the outcome.'* She has provided many case studies and stories such as a new general manager at Daimler-Benz in South Africa who, when faced with sluggish workers, high rates of defects and many lost days of productivity, gave them the project to produce a car for the recently released Nelson Mandela. The result was a reinvigorated workforce who produced a car that was perfectly made in record time. The sense of pride and purpose in this challenge had a direct impact on raising performance levels. Or what about Gillette's Himalayan project that took on the challenge to change the way men shaved in India so they avoided the blood infections caused by rusty blades. She tells us in her book *Evolve* that meaning not money acts as the motivation. Money, she says, *'acts as a score card but does not help people go home each day fulfilled.'*[6]

I love having a bit of time before I start my day to gather my thoughts, run through the day's work, and to simply be. This time is normally found over a cup of coffee near my client's offices in one of the many coffee shop chains that adorn our city. These places are a constant stream of individuals rushing from one place to another, with no time to stop or talk as they order and grab the flat white or the skinny decaf latte. This no time, high-speed behaviour infects everyone around them. In our frenetic capital city, many people have roles that can place them out of the view of the stressed city worker and into the ranks of the invisible. But there is one coffee shop in London's Great Portland Street that no matter how little acknowledgement they receive in return, every member of staff greets you with a *real* smile and an upbeat enquiry as to how you are while they take your hurried order. Their genuine sense of engagement seems to reflect a team happy to be at work, and their positivity is contagious. Yet, their wages put together probably wouldn't match those of some of the individuals that enter their shop. So, recently, as I ordered my coffee (skinny decaf flat white!) at 7.20am, I remarked to the man behind the counter about how happy he and his team always seemed, thanking him for passing this on to me each time I enter. He smiled and said that it was a good place to work. When I asked him what made it good he simply said, 'They listen to us and we can pretty much run things for ourselves.' I asked him if he ever felt fed up with the one-sided interaction. His response was, 'No, not really. My job is to make their day a little bit better and give them back a bit of time.' His understanding of his contribution and link to the 'why' of his work, which saw beyond the potential mundanity that others might perceive, was tangible as well as inspiring.

The power of purpose is underestimated in the workplace as a critical driver of engagement. I have often wondered if tomorrow aliens invaded us and they assessed our corporate world, what they would make of the infinite presentations, spreadsheets and files. Would the reason for what we do be immediately clear or would we be viewed as a race that busied ourselves with meaningless, arbitrary data? A bit harsh maybe, but how often do we find ourselves putting together yet another slide deck without a true sense of the deeper reason? Or working intensely on a piece of work only for it to be shelved because the original request has moved on?

What's the purpose of the mission?

Many businesses have mission or purpose statements, often supported by a list of values, but how many have taken the time to explore the meaning these statements have with those tasked with steering the work in the espoused direction? Jim Collins and Jerry Porras in their book *Built to Last* wrote: '*Core purpose is the organisation's fundamental reason for being, the difference it seeks to make in the world. An effective purpose reflects the importance people attach to the company's work – it taps their idealistic motivation – and gets at the deeper reasons for an organisation's existence beyond just making money.'*

Their book listed some of the most powerful purpose statements from some of the most successful and enduring businesses, all of which deliberately and directly refer to and align the contribution of every employee and strategic move to what they term their higher purpose:

Johnson & Johnson: *'To alleviate pain and suffering.'*

Merck: *'To gain victory against disease and help mankind.'*

Sam Walton, founder of Wal-Mart: *'To give ordinary folk the chance to buy the same thing as rich people.'*

Disney: *'To use our imaginations to bring happiness to millions.'*

Southwest Airlines, as one of the earliest low-cost airlines: *'To give people the freedom to fly.'*

Southwest Airlines has posted a profit every quarter for over 36 years. No other airline comes anywhere near. Their purpose never changed despite huge shifts in the industry, and their work has been attributed to why over 85% of Americans have now travelled by plane.

These grand, huge statements have set these organisations apart, providing an unwavering core ideology around which each has created environments for innovation that every individual can work towards and emotionally attach. Once you can describe the why, the purpose, everything else starts to make sense. Proctor & Gamble's former global marketing officer, Jim Stengel, said, 'Purpose drives an entire organisation and it answers why the brand exists.'

I've worked with numerous teams at all levels and have often posed the question: 'Why does your business exist?' And so often I hear: 'for shareholder value', 'to make money', 'for profit' and so on. So, I rephrase the question and ask: 'If all those things were a given, what do you see as the purpose of the work done here and what are the unwavering values that underpin how and why you deliver that work?' This usually delivers blank faces and a few rolling eyes after which, with a little more coaxing, a valuable discussion starts where groups and individuals explore what their work means to them personally and collectively. I have also been challenged around creating purpose within some roles: 'some jobs are simply without meaning and carried out purely for a wage – aren't they?' One of the key aspects of purpose is the perception that what is done has a lasting impact on others. Take for a moment the following jobs:

- Accountant

- Analyst

- Shelf stacker

Now consider these roles:

- Nurse

- Fire officer

- Police officer

- Teacher

Most individuals can describe the purpose of the latter roles in terms of their significance and impact on society but often find it hard to articulate the meaning within roles such as those in the first list. Maybe if we looked differently at the first list, from the angle of the outcome of the work they carry out. An accountant supports individuals and companies to thrive economically. An analyst makes sense from data that can inform everything from new ways of working to new medicines. The shelf stacker brings order, efficiency and access to products helping the shopper and the retailer achieve what they need. OK, whilst you may agree or disagree with these descriptions, the key is that meaning and purpose can be found in everything we do if we believe in it, whatever the role, and can bring us achievement and pride.

Take the famous story of the cleaner at Nasa who, when asked what he did by John Kennedy, answered, 'Mr President, I'm helping put a man on the moon.' The challenge to our sense of direction comes when employees are too distant from the recipient and benefits of their work to make the link between what they do and why they do it. When university fundraisers met a single student whose scholarship was funded by their work they made a concrete link to the value of what they do. The outcome of this experience saw an increase in weekly phone minutes of 142% and weekly revenue grew by 400%.[7] When radiologists saw a patient's photo included in an x-ray file, they wrote 29% longer reports and made 46% more accurate diagnoses.[8] The closer we are to those our work directly impacts creates a clear line of sight between what we do and the why.

Putting purpose into practice can tackle huge challenges. One such problem is getting the healthcare practitioners in hospitals to wash their hands. It's not that they aren't aware, lack understanding or have not been told of the need for washing their hands as the best way to prevent diseases, but the studies have shown that in practice they only washed their hands, on average, about a third to half the time they came in contact with patients. Adam Grant of the University of Pennsylvania and David Hofman of the University of North Carolina studied the impact of the signs placed over soap dispensers and hand sanitisers. They devised two signs to be placed over the soap and gel dispensers: *Hand hygiene prevents you from catching*

diseases' and *'Hand hygiene prevents patients from catching diseases'.*
Grant, as a psychologist, understood the illusion of invulnerability:
that most of us think the bad stuff will happen to someone else and
don't place ourselves at risk of becoming sick (particularly healthcare
professionals). Grant and Hofman wanted to see if what really shifted
behaviour was the concern for others based on the premise that those
working in healthcare had primarily entered to help others – their
purpose. The sign about the patients increased hand washing and gel
use by 33%.[9] By changing a single word in a sign they had made the
tangible link between hand washing and purpose.

I listened to an interview with Jo Malone, founder and creator of the
eponymous organisation. As she told the story of her journey, she
recounted the sale of her business to Estée Lauder in 1999 – a sound
strategic decision that catapulted the brand and fixed the security of
its founder. Jo exited the business after some time and, as is usual,
signed a no-competition contract that stopped her creating scents or
working for others in this capacity for five years. Jo's passion and the
reason for the business when it began was the creation of fragrance.
Her expertise – built through years of experience and coupled with
a natural flair for mixing ingredients together to create unique
perfumes – was made temporarily redundant. Despite the financial
foundation she'd gained, Jo went on to detail the void that not being
able to pursue her creative work had left – an issue she had not fully
anticipated. She described the lack of purpose to her day and world
without the fulfilment of her passion. She told us of how it negatively
affected her mood and those around her until she could start again
with her new business. A sense of purpose is emotional in nature,
not rational. It needs to make sense to our limbic system before it
can make sense to our conscious executive brain. If we can make the
connections emotionally we will tap into the available neurological
reward, which leads to motivation and focused effort. Purpose is the
reason volunteers continue to volunteer and artists create. A day's

work without purpose is draining. Effort without meaning is simply hard work.

Money does not make meaning

So, can the purpose of work be purely monetary? Working to feed our families and to keep a roof over our heads is purpose – right? The wage packet is an absolute necessity for so many and for others with more disposable income money can support security and fulfil personal ambition. But money in and of itself does not lead to intrinsic neurobiological reward. Purpose, meaning, direction is individual and, whilst money is recompense for work, whether overgenerous, fair or ungenerous, it is an extrinsic factor that has a limited influence on engagement. Gallup's world poll, a survey of the happiness of adults in 132 countries, shows that richer people do not always feel happier. An income beyond $75K per year in the US, £55K per year in the UK, does not equate to any further increments in overall happiness ratings.[10] I of course balance this argument with a recognition that below an income level where essential resources are out of reach the outcome is more likely to be misery.

Paul Dolan, in his book *Happiness by Design*, describes his pleasure-purpose principle. He details how happiness needs to include both pleasure and purpose, and that these are separate components that make up our overall happiness. We are not designed to be happy all the time. We should experience a range of emotions as we interpret and respond appropriately to events and our environment. No job is always completely exciting, but whilst there is mundanity or parts that are less 'fun', you can feel overall happier because of its level of purpose and concomitant reward. I once spoke to a paramedic who explained that his job mostly involved clearing up after drunks at the weekend, none of which was particularly pleasurable, but he continued, 'I could not and would not want to do anything else because what I do makes a difference every day.' It is this sense of reward from the meaning his work gives him that holds his motivation steadfast despite the tough working conditions and the level of pay. To what degree do you consider what you do as worthwhile? What about your team – if they were asked, what answer would they give about the purpose of their work?

Dolan says to be truly happy you need to feel both pleasure and purpose. You may need different degrees at different times, but you need to feel both. Despite the stressful elements, the routine tasks and the taxing politics of your role, if what you are working towards is worth more than the sum of its parts, the result will be strong intrinsic motivation. Yet still so many jobs are designed without the foundation of meaning or the clarity of how and why each role contributes to the overall purpose. It's not, I hope, intentional in design that leaders are actively seeking robots to deliver through meaningless activities in return for a paycheque. After all, if the task itself is meaningless then why does it continue to exist? Or, in other words, if it does exist it must relate to the wider success of the organisation, which means that the individuals carrying out the duties can always understand how and why what they do is purposeful.

So What?

Purpose not money makes the world go round...

Jim Collins, in his book *Good to Great*, notes how: '*Enduring great companies don't exist merely to deliver returns to shareholders. Indeed, in a truly great company, profits and cash flow become like blood and water to a healthy body: they are absolutely essential for life, but they are not the very point of life.*' So what's the formula for the lasting endurance of an organisation? Collins continues: '*To make the shift from a company with sustained great results to an enduring great company of iconic stature… discover your core values and purpose beyond just making money (core ideology) and combine this with the dynamic of preserve the core/stimulate progress.*'[11]

So, this is all well and good but what does that do, if anything, for the bottom line? Jim Stengel of Proctor & Gamble commissioned a study of over 30,000 brands with a focus on the 25 top-performing ones. The in-depth study found that all the top-performing brands were fulfilling a higher order purpose.[12] Furthermore, Collins, over the course of a six-year research project with Jerry Porras,[13] found that long-enduring and highly successful organisations all had a clear sense of purpose built around a core ideology beyond making money that differentiated them and provided meaningful identity to all employees. Once the purpose is set, there needs to be a clear line of sight from each individual employee's contribution to that higher purpose; after that it's down to the individual to choose to connect.

Getting the purpose and connection formula right will go a long way to delivering a motivated workforce and a high-performing business that understands and delivers on its promises. Collins and Porras demonstrated that organisations driven by purpose and values outperformed the general market by 15:1 and outperformed comparison companies 6:1. John Kotter and James Heskett of Harvard Business School studied blue-chip organisations from 20 industries. They found that those with a compelling culture based on core shared values significantly outperformed those with weak or neutral cultures. Their four-year study showed that these companies' revenue grew more than four times faster, while profit performance was significantly higher than comparison companies in the same industries.[14] These are all compelling reasons for a reason, but why does it make such a difference?

Decisions become faster, easier and clearer. For organisations with clear purpose and values, the 'what' and 'why' is accessible. It creates a lens through which the world is viewed and moves are made based on their relevance to and alignment with that viewpoint. Questions such as cut costs, outsource, pursue a different market are simpler to answer if the result of them being put into action would be to violate our purpose. The enduring companies push these questions out of the boardroom window. BMW ignores an automotive technological change if it does not directly support their customers to continue to experience the joy of driving. Bright Horizons discard anything that could, in any way, risk the safety of their young charges. Walt Disney has used its purpose and values to create a decision tree known and understood by every employee. It reads:

1. Safety
2. Courtesy
3. Show
4. Efficiency

In any situation, safety trumps everything and decisions are not only quick but also far more easily justified and understood. As a result, the choices made support consistency in behaviour, creating a solid basis for company culture and protection of the core purpose.

Pay attention!

Our ability to focus and concentrate is depleted when we have low fulfilment. When we are engaged in activities we enjoy, are competent at, and provide us with meaning and direction, we tune out distractions. Mihaly Csikszentmihalyi, leading researcher in positive psychology, describes this feeling of time flying by without us realising as 'flow'. When in flow we are fully absorbed, engrossed. Richard Davidson, neuroscientist of the University of Wisconsin, finds that during sharp focus, such as a state of flow, key circuitry of the pre-frontal cortex is synchronised with the object of awareness. He calls this phase 'locking' and has shown how this strengthens our learning. The more our mind wanders, the less we hold our focus and the more holes we get in our learning. The constant stream of information and interruption that bombards our working lives further exacerbates the demands on our attention. It's a wonder that we get anything done.

Attention Economics examines human attention as a scarce resource. Herbert A. Simon first describes the challenge with our attention as follows: '...in an information-rich world, the wealth of information means a dearth of something else: a scarcity of whatever it is that information consumes. What information consumes is rather obvious: it consumes the attention of its recipients. Hence a wealth of information creates a poverty of attention and a need to allocate that attention efficiently among the overabundance of information sources that might consume it.'[15]

Attention is obviously a crucial resource for business. Purpose enhances attention and delivers returns. The psychologist Daniel Goleman shows that people are in flow relatively rarely in daily life. Sampling people at random reveals that most of the time people are either stressed or bored. Only 20% of people have flow moments at least once a day. Around 15% of people never enter a flow state during a typical day. He writes: 'We get a doorway to flow from just manageable tasks that challenge our abilities and doing what we are passionate about. So up a sense of purpose and add some pressure.'[16]

The meaning of life

A purpose answers a need in the world. Where there is a need there is a market, and where there is a service or product that meets the needs of the market, profits, growth and hopefully societal good is the result. It's not rocket science, but leaders who understand a need of the world in which they can bring and apply knowledge, even before the people in it recognise it as a need, can start to build an organisation. Sam Walton, founder of Wal-Mart, saw the need for people in rural America to have access to good quality products without paying higher than average prices just because of where they lived. He set out to deliver on his promise to change this and continues to do so without compromise. Purpose directs and unites people through a common reason and desire to progress, which provides that intrinsic reward.

It is not just at an organisational level that purpose delivers, it does so at an individual level too. Research reviewing data from ten studies investigating the relationship between purpose in life, mortality and cardiovascular events involving over 136,000 men and women, carried out in 2015 by Dr Randy Cohen and colleagues, found that people with a high sense of purpose, direction and meaning – as measured by psychological surveys – had a 23% reduction in mortality and 19% reduction in cardiovascular events as opposed to individuals with a low sense of purpose. Furthermore, regardless of the individual's country or the definition of their purpose, the effect was consistent.[17] Cohen et al.'s conclusions were that possessing a high sense of purpose in life is associated with a reduced risk for all-cause mortality and cardiovascular events.

A study published in The Lancet looking at subjective wellbeing and aging – the analysis of the English Longitudinal Study of Ageing – identified that eudaemonic wellbeing (sense of purpose and meaning in life) is associated with increased survival: 29.3% of people in the lowest wellbeing quartile died during the average follow-up period of 8.5 years compared with 9.3% of those in the highest quartile. Associations were independent of age, sex, demographic factors, and baseline mental and physical health.[18] The Rush Memory and Ageing project has released four studies in which they tested participants on an annual basis and through organ donation after their death. The results are striking, showing that subjects who scored higher on the purpose scale were 52% less likely to develop Alzheimer's disease, 44% less likely to have a stroke and to be 2.5 times more likely to not develop dementia.

So, why is a direction with purpose so protective? It feels intuitively correct. To live my life daily in pursuit of things that carry meaning not only clarifies my choices but also gives me the reason to embrace the day. We often hear that someone is following a calling or entering a vocation, not a job. But still, why is it so protective? Well the answer lies in the chemicals. Neurochemicals associated with reward, such as serotonin, are psychologically and physiologically protective. They work to motivate us to pursue and do more of the same actions that trigger the reward system. Studies have shown that having a higher sense of purpose is associated with lower levels of the stress hormone cortisol,[19] which over time is physically and mentally destructive. Challenging yourself regularly to pursue things that strengthen a sense of purpose, which in turn reinforces behaviours that build self-esteem, on the other hand, increases serotonin. Purpose, as part of our neurobiological reward system, meant that we banded together for and didn't give up on the shared goals required to obtain the resources we needed for survival and adaptation. No different for projects at work.

One's sense of purpose can be tested at retirement. The marketing for retirement often centres on it being the space to do all the things you never had time for and that life will be better, but it can lead to a loss of identity, diminished motivation and concerns over financial security. Finding a renewed sense of purpose beyond work is vital to stave off harmful effects on both mental and physical health. Okinawa in Japan is one of the nine 'Blue Zones' – cultures studied because inhabitants live measurably longer and healthier lives. A sense of purpose is amongst the aspects all the Blue Zones have in common. In the Okinawan language there is not a word for retirement; instead they have 'ikigai', translated as 'the reason for being'. The Blue Zones project lists a sense of purpose as worth up to seven years of extra life expectancy.[20]

There is no singular defined sense of purpose; it is personal and can come in many guises, from family to sport to volunteering to craft to health research and so on. Every purpose carries a clear direction and meaning for the individual. It is what we do today and what we work towards tomorrow. It provides focus, motivation and a reason to be and do. As a colleague reminded me, we are Human Beings, not Human Doings.

What if...

Translating purpose, meaning and direction into the workplace should be a vital part of any communication and leadership approach. There are many ways and I hope that the following suggestions will spark ideas that work for you.

What if... we linked individual and team contribution to the outcome? Leaders can leverage the intrinsic motivation from purpose by creating clarity – through discussion and debate with their teams – around the purpose of each and every role. This purpose can be related to business as usual, the team objectives, a specific change or project or the overarching organisation's direction and contribution to society. Detailing the value of every role allows individuals to establish their own sense of meaning and connection, deepening their desire to contribute to the group success. Work on articulating the 'why you do' before the 'what you do'.

Making the job meaningful to others and society – finding the link and communicating how the organisation impacts and positively supports the wider social context – is critical. Get employees closer to the end user/recipient. This is why leaders at John Deere invite employees who build tractors to meet the farmers who buy their tractors; why leaders at Facebook invite software developers to hear from users who have found long-lost friends and family members thanks to the site; and why leaders at Wells Fargo film videos of customers describing how low-interest loans have rescued them from debt.

What if... we really linked our personal values to our work? Values are individual and have a distinct definition for their owner – as do organisational values. Employees will hold intrinsic values that leaders and businesses cannot and should not try to change to make a fit. When we work against our values we lose motivation. Our values have been established over our lifetime, shaped by our experiences to create rules by which we live and interact. Think for a moment about something that you hold as fundamentally important – family, health, learning etc. Think of something that you would hold true to, irrespective of whether you were rewarded or paid for it in some way, something that if you no longer had to work, you would continue to live your life accordingly. Ask yourself how you feel when the value you have chosen is being compromised in some way. And how do you feel when this value is fully supported, when it is present and thriving? If you notice negative and positive emotional responses to these questions respectively then you are on track to understanding your values. See if you can write a list of your values and from that list pick out the top five. Over the next few weeks, note when you feel at ease, energised, comfortable: which values are being supported? This exercise helps to define personal values and to bring them to self-awareness. Knowing your values smooths decisions when faced with choices. Think of Disney's decision tree and apply something similar to your world.

Now perhaps you could ask yourself in relation to your work:

- Do I value what my role and what my organisation stands for?

- Do I know what my organisation's real purpose is?

- Can I see the direct link between what I do every day and the purpose of my organisation?

- Can I articulate the link between my team's roles and the organisation's purpose?

How could your organisation work to uncover its true values, its key attributes and strengths – those elements that whatever the future holds will remain steadfast and support a clear purpose? Strategies, policies and processes can change but the purpose of and the values by which work is done are unwavering. Trying to create and force a values list of honourable words without deeper exploration and understanding of the 'why' does not work. The words stand as empty symbols that can lead to divide and dissatisfaction if they are not felt or experienced.

What if... as part of the recruitment phase articulating and exploring the values of the organisation and the fit with prospective employee's values is carried out? A Match.com approach to recruitment.

What if... the organisation's values and purpose are used to create decision shortcuts? Does what you are looking to do uphold your purpose?

What if... we look at the day-to-day behaviours within the organisation; do they support or undermine the core values and organisation's purpose?

What if... you ask your clients and suppliers to describe your purpose and the values they see you upholding in their interaction with you?

What if... we put our money where our mouth is? If you truly believe in the why and how then let your clients and customers know not to pay if there is anything that doesn't fit. It builds trust in the brand. One example of this is the growing market for 'pay-what-it's-worth' restaurants. A business model that doesn't charge for the food but based on a clear purpose and belief in the quality of the food, service and overall customer experience allows customers to work out their own bill, a strategy that screams risk but is proving to be very successful. Peter Ilic set up his restaurant Just Around the Corner over 30 years ago with exactly this approach. Sold to and now run by Michael Vasos, Vasos continues to make more money with this business than his other four fixed-price menu restaurants. This, of course, plays into other factors such as the integrity, honesty and fairness of the customers, as well as their desire to not offend; and of course, can open the restaurant up for abuse – but all the more reason for focusing on the purpose through every action and every bite.

Einstein once *wrote: 'It would be possible to describe everything scientifically… but it would make no sense, it would be without meaning as if you described a Beethoven symphony as a variation of wave pressure.'*

Does your workplace create the real sense of purpose, direction and meaning or is it simply people coming in every day without connection? Do you see the repeated oscillations of waves on a screen or do you hear the symphony?

CHAPTER 3
RELATIVE POSITION

*'Before God we are equally wise –
and equally foolish.'*

Albert Einstein

The What...

Have you ever been in a meeting when no matter what you say no one really listens and your voice seems to float on the outside of the room, your opinions seemingly of no importance or relevance for others? Or maybe you have had a job where you have sensed a social divide between it and other roles? Or have you experienced or witnessed discrimination simply because geographical and evolutionary history has led to a different adaptation in skin colour? Or what about that company restructure that requests you reapply for your position, justifying your skills and value for the possibility that you can remain? How do these examples affect our sense of significance and position relative to others?

The green-eyed monster

In every conversation, every interaction, we assess our perceived significance and relative position to another or within the group or the community in which we live and work. Are we heard? Is there any perceived difference in our standing? At work do people look to us for advice from our field of knowledge? Do others recognise the value of the contribution we make – do they even know what we do? What do you feel when you hear the words 'Let me give you some feedback'? Six little words placed as the precursor to a problem. A reduced perception of our position to others triggers our threat circuitry, leaving us feeling vulnerable to those higher up the significance ladder. We can allow envy to creep in as we define our social standing based on what we have or have not compared to others. Envy raises its ugly head when we believe we have come up short. This only serves to knock our self-esteem which is closely linked to our comparison of how we view ourselves against our ideal self, and often, instead of motivating us to work harder, brings on behaviour that damages relationships.

Knowing the value of what we bring to the team and the recognition of that value being reciprocated is neurologically rewarding for a very good reason: to ensure we continue to contribute. Our relative position provides us with clarity of our significance to the group that in turn represents our continued inclusion. Teams, communities and groups work best when complementary skills, strengths and experience combine to deliver on a shared goal. Skills-based cooperation has a strong evolutionary benefit but with a condition: that no single individual is putting in more than another. We need reciprocal altruism. Individuals who don't have anything to offer, free-loading as they take up scarce resources, become a source of resentment for others who are working hard to achieve. That resentment can turn into attitudes of exclusion – and exclusion, as we will see in the next chapter, is a major source of threat for us.

It's all a question of rank

So, back to those first scenarios. My expectation is that as you read the opening paragraph you felt anything from mild irritation to anger depending on what experience this might have tapped into. These emotions are a primary response to threat, a signal to the body that action is required to defend ourselves. This mechanism is so innate in us it can be triggered simply by a line in a book that describes the undermining of an individual's relevance and importance. When we perceive a diminished sense of significance, this threat response can lead to unhelpful behaviours such as withdrawal, anger, sarcasm and a myriad of other actions that seek to reinstate our position and to avoid potential social exclusion. This stems from the fear that we are not seen as worthy enough to be a part of the group. The focus on this threat will distract our minds from work as our brains try to solve the issue.

Can you remember a time when you felt ignored, were slighted by another or were patronised – how long did this stay with you as you turned the event over in your mind? Have you ever done this to another? Have you ever witnessed or experienced a boss undermining an idea or effort? I remember in my second job at the age of 19 my boss shouted, criticised and demanded – nothing was ever good enough. My colleague and I were the lowest of the low, making her toast in the morning and sometimes having to redo it if the butter was not spread evenly enough. It shattered my self-confidence. My only respite was Friday nights since the dread of going back in on Monday started to affect me on Saturday. My colleague and I retreated, supporting each other in our shared trauma. Sounds dramatic? For me at the time it was all consuming and, ironically, as my confidence fell, mistakes crept into my performance, which led to my boss laying into me further, perpetuating a downward spiral of both wellbeing and performance.

I now know that she was a bully and bullies are in their own eyes inadequate. As they undermine others they are perversely trying to raise their own perceived status. I would be far better equipped today to handle the situation, not internalising it as I did then, instead placing the blame back at her door. These were her issues not mine. I didn't have the tools to cope back then, but I did have the courage to leave. It's a tough lesson but one that has helped me to connect, at least to a certain extent, to the impact of a perception of shattered sense of relative position and significance. As Maya Angelou so rightly says, 'People will forget what you said, people will forget what you did, but people will never forget how you made them feel.'

I have seen many examples of undermined significance at work, from refusing a holiday request, delivering feedback as if telling off a child, individuals extolling their own achievements in a hope to bolster their position, to power plays being made around individual agendas. So, whilst a sense of recognised value and significance is motivating, the opposite is a threat and leads to disengagement, reduced performance and business risk.

Primatologist Robert Sapolsky has studied baboon social behaviour for over three decades. Like us, baboons are intelligent, organised and face only a few physical stressors. They only have to work for about three hours a day to get their food and most predators don't mess with them. What his work has shown is that baboons get diseases that other social animals don't generally have. The trouble appears to be the spare time baboons have, during which they devote a great deal of energy to generating psychosocial stress towards others in their troop. He says, 'If you're a gazelle, you don't have a very complex emotional life, despite being a social species. But primates are just smart enough that they can think their bodies into working differently. It's not until you get to primates that you get things that look like depression… so the baboon is a wonderful model for living well enough and long enough to pay the price for all the social-stressor nonsense that they create for each other. They're just like us: if they're not getting done in by predators and famines, they're getting done in by each other.'

One of Sapolsky's early findings was to establish the link between stress and hierarchy. Like us, baboons have evolved large brains that enable them to navigate the complexities of social structures. Those within the troops that sit at the top of the social ranks have the pick of the females, all the food they wish, and groomers ready and willing at their beck and call. Every male understands his position within the troop: who will dominate him, who he can dominate and so on. Sapolsky found that a baboon's rank determined the level of stress hormones in his system. The greater your dominance and social position, the lower your stress hormones, but if the baboon is submissive they will be much higher. Additionally, the lower ranks had increased blood pressure and heart rates, which in turn depleted their health and showed similarities to a clinically depressed human. Overall his studied troop was typical in their behaviour: the males were aggressive, society was highly stratified, and the females took the brunt of male dominance. What happened next to the troop, however, was to profoundly affect the path of research.

The baboons Sapolsky had grown close to ate meat thrown out by a tourist lodge. The meat was tainted with tuberculosis and the result was that over half the males died. Whilst seemingly catastrophic for the troop, Sapolsky started to study the baboons that had died and those that had not. What he found was that if you were higher ranking, aggressive and not particularly socially connected or affiliative you died. First dibs on the toxic food were for the higher status males. Left were twice as many females as males and the males that survived were in Sapolsky's words the 'good guys'. They were socially affiliative and nice to the females. The culture of the troop completely changed. Even when new adolescent male baboons joined the troop, bringing their learnt aggression with them, they eventually assimilated to this very different, less aggressive, socially supporting environment. And this troop is living this way 20 years later, not just surviving but thriving. The tragedy provided Sapolsky with a new platform to study the impact of aggressive hierarchy on stress through the absence of it. These baboons do not have the same problems with heart rate, blood pressure or stress hormone levels. So, what can this teach us? We don't need to dominate to achieve. Social affiliation and altruism is far more powerful. And yet the pursuit of power appears to drive our western world – so can we really change?

So What?

Our sense of self-worth is profoundly influenced by the degree to which we perceive how others rank and value us.

'It is not just your rank but what your rank means to your society.'
R Sapolsky

The psychologist Daniel Goleman wrote: *'Threats to our standing in the eyes of others are remarkably potent biologically, almost as powerful as those to our very survival. After all, the unconscious equation goes, if we are judged to be undesirable, we may not only be shamed, but suffer complete rejection.'* [21]

Is this need for significance universal? There has been some research done on emotional expression of pride to signify our social significance. In 2008, Jess Tracy and David Matsumoto carried out a study on the emotional expressions of winning and losing in the body language of Olympiads at the 2004 Athens Games. They found that across the cultures the same expression of pride was used: expanding the chest, clenching the fists, placing the arms on the hips or raising them upwards in a V shape, with a small controlled smile. Their study included congenitally blind athletes who also showed the same pattern of pride display. Their results seem to indicate that displays of success such as these are not just mimicked or socially accepted norms but part of an evolved communication of one's socially valued place. [22] Winning in all walks of life raises our social rank and value through a demonstration of skill, strengths and expertise, and perhaps because someone else has, by default, lost. In the absence of formal hierarchy, groups form themselves around the skills they have and often a natural leader is appointed, a role which itself is an identified skills match. There is usually a 'go-to' person in any group. A leader is often recognised through a higher perception of position relative to others, but this should not be to the detriment of any other member of the team's sense of significance and position therein.

Value every position in the team

The efficiency and performance gains delivered from leveraging the intrinsic motivator for significance and position is played out in different settings. When you watch the roughly two and a half seconds it takes for a Formula 1 pit-stop team to change four wheels you can see how each individual has a specific task and position. Whilst as a team they have rehearsed the actions many times, the foundation of the process has been established through clear individual contribution, position and significance to each other. Each part working together to create the whole. This valued contributor approach has been brought home through Atul Guwande's work[23] in surgical theatres. Through his research into high performance he learned about the power of checklists from lessons experienced in aviation. Despite expertise and experience, we can overlook the basics as pressure rises or we rely on (and forgive the pun) autopilot. But rigorously, consciously applied checklists mitigate the risk of missing crucial yet seemingly obvious and thus forgettable tasks.

The checklists brought in by Guwande start before the operation and take the surgical team through the procedure up until the point when the patient leaves the operating theatre. Checks are made before the anaesthetic is administered, before the knife hits the skin, and even to ensure that the right patient is on the table. One major check asks for each person to introduce himself or herself at the start of the day and detail the expertise and role they provide. These surgical teams are often brought together for the first time at the point of surgery and making sure that every person's role is understood and recognised may seem obvious but was often missed. Guwande's checklist has been implemented in eight hospitals around the globe and, so far, the complication rates in surgery have fallen by 35% and death rates have fallen by an astounding 47%, a remarkable and hugely important outcome. Not only does his work provide clear evidence for the power of checklists to create pause moments in a process to catch a problem before it occurs, it specifically gives space for every individual to state and be valued for their significance to the team.

I referred to aviation as being a source of Guwande's research. The lessons learnt about the importance of perceived significance and relative position by this industry were extremely harsh. Air crashes have been caused through deference to authority. Individuals have not spoken up when things are going wrong because of the psychological barrier of hierarchical role. One such devastating air crash was on 27 March 1977 at Tenerife airport, when an aircraft smashed into another on the runway, killing 585 people. Two perfectly serviceable airplanes collided in fog. The voice recordings in the cockpit minutes before the disaster revealed that one of the key reasons for the crash was the authority grading between the captain and the co-pilot and engineer. The captain was very senior and was described as having a 'god-like' persona, which worked against him as the crew, who knew that the plane did not have clearance to take off, were overruled by him during the take-off run, leading him straight into another aircraft's path. When investigated it became clear that this authority issue was widespread across the industry, leading co-pilots, engineers, crew members and others to delay speaking up, challenging or even taking over when they recognised errors being made by senior figures. As one investigating psychologist said at the time, 'Co-pilots would rather die than contradict a captain.'

Over the past 30 years the aviation industry has focused on training to overcome this problem, but it was the Kegworth air crash in 1989 that was the real game changer. A Boeing 737 on a routine flight from Belfast to London crashed into the embankment on the M1 after one of its engines malfunctioned. The voice recordings showed that the pilots quickly diagnosed the issue but they shut down the wrong engine. The captain announced to the passengers and crew that he had shut down the right-hand engine. At that time, there was a 'them and us' culture between the pilots and the perceived lower status cabin crew who had been told not to interrupt the pilots in a crisis. Investigation showed that the cabin crew could see that the left-hand engine was on fire but they didn't say anything. It seems extraordinary that those in the cabin worked out the error but said nothing simply because of their perception of the pilot's greater position. The brain's perceived threat of breaking rank was too great. The aviation industry has now brought in compulsory training in assertiveness to teach all employees how to listen and to speak up in situations where error is made. A common language has been established, which is now respected by all levels of employee and provides a path to communicate issues. In amongst this standardised unambiguous language are certain crisis trigger words that cut through the pressure and any blockers of rank. These are: 'I am **uncomfortable**'; 'I am **concerned**'; 'This is **unsafe**'; 'We need to **stop**'. These simple words provide a safe space to speak up overcoming the potential neurological threat from differences in relative position.

Value every person's contribution

John Harsanyi, who won the Nobel Memorial prize in economic sciences, is quoted as saying, 'Apart from economic payoffs, social status seems to be the most important incentive and motivating force of social behaviour.' The process of creating a functioning group where everyone's contribution is understood and fits in neatly to complete the overall team puzzle is often painful. The 'Storming-Norming-Forming-Performing' process is widely known in the workplace and recognises the normal behaviours of people as they jostle to find their fit. Our significance and position is not all about being top dog; it is far more about being valued and recognised for the specialism and strengths we bring. In a well-structured team, everyone from the admin clerk, to the cleaner, to the CEO is a part of the overall running of the workplace, but so often the perceived social divide causes problems. I remember a senior partner at a top professional services firm, as I explained this contribution matrix approach, commenting that in life some jobs are simply more important than others. He voiced a genuine belief that the administrators in his team were not as significant as the managers or him because of the level of skill required and the basic level of the tasks they carried out. My counter argument is not that roles that carry greater risk and require higher skill and experience should not be recognised (and traditionally status, remuneration and benefits are the recognition), but that if a job or a task is not important, not needed for the desired goal, then why does it exist? If it has a place then it should be clearly valued as such and also the contribution of the person delivering on that role. All roles at work should be respected and should not be used to either devalue or overinflate the person carrying out any one role. Walking past each other in a supermarket aisle a CEO and a clerk are equals as they choose which peas to buy.

The bias around the social standing of professions can lead to disparity of significance and that's when the problems arise. Not so long ago many organisations, including one I worked for, called the internal accounting functions the 'back-office'. It might as well have been called the Oubliette for the lack of value that was placed on the work done by the teams. Yet support functions provide a foundation for the whole business. Terms such as 'business partner' have come in and have played a part in closing the status gap, but the divide is still there in many organisations and, as in society, prejudicial behaviour can act to magnify the gap. I've often heard statements such as 'we are just the second-class citizens' from those working in these areas in a business where the perception is that the role is not as good or as worthy as others. Result: demotivation.

Social ranking

As divides in perceived significance grow and our relative position to others shrinks, the more it becomes a subject of focus for the individuals involved. Materialistic consumerism is an example of how we visually proclaim our social position, with loud brands and labels that shout 'I have more' and presumably somewhere therein, a need to say 'and you have less'. Research by psychologist P J Henry at De Paul University detailed what he called 'low-status compensation' theory. His studies explored the higher rates of self-protectionism in low-status groups as compared to high-status groups. Those that perceive themselves as low-status amplify this position to front of mind and place a focus on the associated threats within their environment. Because of their vigilance, they are quicker to defend and protect their sense of self-worth – even doing so violently. In fact, Henry's research started examining groups that were in the lower status role of herdsmen versus those in the higher position of farmers. He showed that the murder rates were higher in the areas where herding was prominent. Even after accounting for levels of general wealth in any one county (higher wealth areas have lower murder rates), the status divides still predicted murder rates.

He then followed up this initial observation by researching data from across 92 different countries to show the same pattern of low-status increases in violence. In his continued study he surveyed 1,500 Americans, the results of which showed that those with perceived low socio-economic status reported higher levels of self-reported defensiveness, believing they were more likely to be taken advantage of and in turn had less trust in others.[24] Individuals with this level of stigma surrounding their perceived low social standing tend to continually make a point, both verbally and seemingly physically, about the divide, reacting strongly to any suggestion of discrimination or the potential risk of such. This stalwart position serves to reinforce the perception of lower status both in themselves and others, which can lead to a self-fulfilling prophecy and has an impact on their economic, mental and social wellbeing. Psychologist Adam Waytz of Northwestern University has research that supports this. He says that *'when a person feels low social status, he or she tends to act in ways that negate efforts to increase status leaving individuals and groups to fall victim to their perception, deserving their place in society and whilst defending it do nothing to change it.'* Waytz's work with Eugene Caruso of the University of Chicago and others showed that just the mere exposure to money affects people's endorsement of social systems that legitimise social inequality, demonstrating how thinking about money can influence beliefs about social order, dictating how deserving one feels of one's station in life.

The holding of social station can serve to build protective walls around groups. From a survival perspective, this probably served us well as we looked to manage the resources we had using the relevant skills within our group to prosper – but at what cost to other groups identified as of a different social significance and position? History and the present provide us with many examples of this, from the ousting of the Aboriginals in Australia, Hitler's quest for Aryan supremacy, and the disgrace of the South African apartheid. We have all witnessed and experienced situations where our significance is diminished, while probably at some points also been guilty of using our perceived greater power over others. Take the waiter going unnoticed by the diner, the school child teasing another because of the colour of their hair or the clothes they are wearing, or the boss reprimanding a new graduate for a mistake.

As Robert Fuller describes, we have all felt like somebody and nobody at points in our lives. The situation itself can shift our sense of relative position: we can perhaps be somebody with our friends but nobody in that meeting at work. In his book *Somebodies and Nobodies,*[25] Fuller examines what he calls Rankism: the abuse of one's rank as an assault on the dignity of others perceived to be of lower rank. In his view, Rankism is the umbrella under which other 'isms' are incubated – sexism, racism and so on. Whatever the reason for being overlooked, when it happens to us our energy is diverted to worrying about it, defending our position and our right to be. When we place another individual lower than ourselves we reduce our empathy for them, objectifying and so justifying why we can be afforded the greater rewards of our rank – whether that be at work or in a community outside.

I remember my first boss who was a kind man but placed himself above all those who had not been privately educated and did not belong to certain societal circles and, as a result, was often heard openly criticising those outside his own definition of what was worthy. Interestingly, at the time not one of his employees had had the privilege of such an education and while it was accepted as just 'his way', he was unwittingly diminishing the value of everyone who worked hard for him. My maiden name was Bennett and I was only 17 when I first started working in his accountancy practice. He could not and did not really try to remember my name so called me Gordon because he made the link between my surname and the outrageous 19th century journalist Gordon Bennett, whose name is often used as an expletive. I didn't like this but I also didn't question it, partly because of my youth but also because I accepted the higher rank he carried in life both as my elder and boss. Presumably he agreed with this difference in level, as otherwise I'd like to think he'd have bothered to remember my name. Try this today, mind you, and there would be a different outcome! I went from him to the bully I mentioned earlier, so my battle scars were formed early in my career. A piece of advice from my mother stood me in good stead, 'No matter what, remember who you are, your strengths, your friends, and how much you are loved, and use this to stand tall.' My sense of significance and self is within me, but that's not to say I don't still feel the impact when it is tested.

Research carried out with police officers showed that those with a sense of higher social standing had better biophysical responses to stress than officers who viewed themselves with lower standing within society. Specifically, higher testosterone, healthier cardiovascular rate and better cardio efficiency enabled the officers to have a more adaptive and effective response to stress. The researchers went further and with a second experiment they showed the link between social significance and beneficial health responses wasn't just correlational.

They determined the social status of the subjects by randomly assigning them high and low status roles. Then in partnerships, one leader and the other supporter, they were asked to work on a fast paced and complex video game together. The higher status subjects exhibited adaptive physiological responses which meant they were better positioned to manage stress, performing better overall. Where we place ourselves, and where we are placed within the levels of society, has a direct impact on how well we respond to stress, relate to others and perform.[26]

F Scott Fitzgerald: 'The rich are different to you and me.'

Ernest Hemingway: 'Yes, they have more money.'

Social standing is also clearly represented in age-old class structures. Class is now perhaps the politically incorrect terminology, but it still exists either formally or informally in societies creating divide. These divides are factors in determining a range of things, from an individual's sense of entitlement to expected social normative behaviour. Social class can be rendered through birth 'right', educational attainment, occupational status or income. Research has shown that those stationed in the lower classes have less educational attainment, poorer health and greater levels of depression – not exactly unsurprising. But what is interesting is that studies have shown that within these classes people have greater empathy and show more altruism. Without certain resources, you need to depend on others.

Knowledge is power?

Letting go and sharing knowledge, while it creates a stronger team over time, can be perceived as a potential threat to our standing particularly if, as with many businesses, restructuring and change has been the name of the game for some time. In the face of the perceived threat from change we too often hold on to what we identify with our social position. We keep our knowledge, defending our position against those that may take away our illusionary power or undermine our significance to the organisation. This creates blockages to information flow and strengthens the gap in relative position, which in turn deepens the sense of threat within the system. Think about this in mergers and acquisitions. The very knowledge that held our significance and position steady can become obsolete. Holding on to knowledge is a natural defence tactic in the face of vulnerability to our significance and can lead good people to leave even before any formal restructuring has started. A study of 180,000 individual workers in more than 800 firms in the face of a merger or acquisition used their perceived comparison of their present status with their future expected status in determining whether to exit or stay.[27] In the face of a merger or acquisition, performance is disrupted as we block knowledge transfer, pushing away intruders in the ensuing culture clash. The whole process slows and starts to drift as we jostle to establish our place and standing. Mismanagement and a lack of understanding of the human reaction to change is a critical reason for why study after study show that most mergers and acquisitions fail to deliver on their original strategy and over half destroy shareholder value.

A place where everyone knows your name

For me what has greater relevance is not the macro look at social divide but the impact on us at the level of micro-moments and face-to-face relationships. The pursuit of social significance and standing is a fundamental factor for human motivation, but the impact on our subjective wellbeing is far greater when respect and recognition comes from our friends, family, colleagues and community. Within our local groups, standing is based on peer respect and admiration rather than income or wealth.[28] This reflection of our significance by those around us provides acceptance and a sense of personal power, both of which are critical determinants of psychological wellbeing.[29] Think about a group of friends or family, or perhaps a team you work with where you feel valued and respected. How does this deepen your sense of belonging, sense of being heard, and feeling of trust? How motivated are you to support them?

Four studies carried out by Cameron Anderson, Michael Kraus and colleagues looked at this local social standing impact, calling it the 'Local Ladder Effect'. In one study, they asked participants to rate their self-perceived status within the local groups they identified as belonging to, using questions such as 'Others admire me'; 'Others look up to me'; 'I have social standing'. They took into consideration the number of leadership positions the participants had held and analysed family income, taking all the data and comparing it with results from running the 'Satisfaction with Life Scale'. The results consistently showed evidence that local standing with face-to-face groups significantly predicted life satisfaction. Longitudinally, as local standing rose or fell, subjective wellbeing also rose or fell, and these effects were driven by feelings of power and social acceptance. This translates directly into the workplace and the teams in which we work. The position and significance of my role, the recognition of my contribution and qualities I bring, as they are understood by my peers and my manager, will have a major influence on my day-to-day motivation.

The abuse of power

An exploration of our relative social position would not be complete without including one of the most infamous psychology experiments – The Stanford Prison Experiment.[30] In 1971, Philip Zimbardo and his team set out to explore the psychological effects of becoming a prisoner, what it was to be a prison guard, and if playing these roles would shift individual behaviours. It was funded by the US Office of Naval Research and stemmed from a need to understand whether the brutality reported across American prisons by prison guards was due to the guards' personality or if it was a situational effect of the prison environment. The experiment was organised to last two weeks but was stopped after only five days by Christine Maslac (at the time a fellow PhD, later to become an eminent psychologist and Zimbardo's wife) due to the severity of the impact on the participants.

Zimbardo used the campus of Stanford University to create a prison. The area was made to look every inch a prison and those to be the guards and those to be the prisoners were randomly selected from male student volunteers. On 17 August, nine of the participant students were arrested without warning, searched, handcuffed and put into police cars. They were taken to the police station, had their fingerprints recorded and were then transported to the Stanford County Prison, aka Stanford University psychology department. This process meant that those who were to be prisoners didn't voluntarily come into the department and surrender their freedom. A priest was enrolled and each day in the prison was meticulously planned in terms of detail. The prisoners were stripped, deloused, and had all their personal possessions removed. They were issued with a uniform, had a locked chain around one ankle and a prison ID number intended to make them feel anonymous. They were from that moment called only by their ID number and had to refer to each other in the same way. The guards were all dressed in the same uniform, had a whistle, a 'billy club', and wore sunglasses to avoid direct eye contact with the prisoners. The guards were instructed to do whatever they felt or thought necessary to keep order, but no physical violence was permitted. What followed has since been described by Zimbardo as one of the most repulsive things he has ever done.

The students playing the guards and those playing the prisoners become subsumed in their roles. The guards, working in sets of three in eight-hour shifts, were creative in using tools to humiliate the prisoners. They harassed, taunted and dehumanised the prisoners, giving them pointless tasks and punishments. The prisoners accepted what was dealt and as they became more submissive the guards became ever more aggressive. One prisoner had to be removed after 36 hours as his thinking became disorganised and he appeared to be entering the early stages of deep depression. In the next couple of days three more had to be removed showing signs of emotional disorder. One of Zimbardo's key mistakes was to enter the role-play himself. He gave himself the role of the prison superintendent, clouding his judgment and view.

Whilst this experiment has, quite rightly, been severely criticised, it provided an insight into how we can conform to social roles and how those roles with a perceived higher social position can award the possessor supposed rights and controls over others lower down the ranks, leading them to abuse their position by objectifying those beneath. One student who played a guard said, 'I practically considered the prisoners cattle,' and one notably said, 'Acting authoritatively can be fun. Power can be great fun,' indicating the neurological reward he was getting at the time of his supremacy. Most of the guards said they found it difficult to believe that they had behaved in such brutal ways and the prisoners were surprised at how readily they became submissive. Zimbardo has since defined evil as the exercise of power.

Whilst there are gaping holes throughout this experiment, we have seen this abuse of power and objectification of others throughout history such as the atrocities carried out by guards in Nazi concentration camps and Abu Ghraib. Stanley Milgrim in 1963 carried out yet another infamous experiment to try to answer the question as to whether the guards involved in the genocides during World War II were merely following orders, a defence given repeatedly at the Nuremburg trials. Milgrim used pairs of subjects, one placed in the role as the learner (and was in fact an ally of Milgrim's team) and the other the teacher. The learner had been given pairs of words to remember and the teacher was asked to test them on these. The two had been introduced to each other but were in separate rooms for the experiment. The learner had been strapped to an electric chair and the teacher was told to administer an electric shock when the learner got an answer wrong and to increase the shock level on each mistake. The learner (who didn't actually receive a shock but could be heard screaming as they acted out the pain) would deliberately give many wrong answers. When teachers refused to give the shock the researcher who sat with the teacher would simply and calmly provide prompts for them to continue. These were: *Please continue; The experiment requires you to continue; It is absolutely essential that you continue; You have no other choice but to continue.* 65% of the teachers continued to deliver shocks, some up to the maximum of 450 volts. Milgrim carried out 18 different versions of this study. His conclusions are that people are likely to follow orders given by those that they see are in authority positions. He called this the 'agentic state' when people allow others to direct their actions and then pass off responsibility for the consequences to the person giving orders.

I fully appreciate that these experiments and explorations of the worst of human acts are both extreme and contain many variables that open them up to ethical criticism, but they demonstrate how the perception we have of our own relative position to that of others can affect how we think and behave. How often do you see a devolvement of responsibility simply because 'they told us' or 'it's come from above'? How many times have you seen an abuse of authority and position, whether that is an inappropriate command style order or someone vocally belittling a role seen to be of less significance? Using rank as a weapon of choice, we can choose to hide behind authority to avoid responsibility or we can abuse our seniority and rank by objectifying those we see at lower stations within the organisation; neither do anything other than demotivate and poison the environment.

The effect of hierarchy

The essence of this chapter is to describe and provide evidence for the neurological reward from recognition by others and our perception of our significance and relative position within our team or community.

We need to know that we are contributing and bring identified skills and qualities to the group so we can share the appropriate resources and spoils from the outcome of the work put in. But hierarchy is not the enemy, it is the abuse of it that is the problem. W.L. Gore is an example of an organisation that has achieved the balance between hierarchy and egalitarian structures. Gore is a privately-owned company and remains highly successful and innovative. Formed in 1958 in the garage of Bill Gore and his wife, the company was set up from the start with a lattice structure approach. There is no formal chain of command, no organisational chart, just a self-regulated collective. Leaders are appointed for different projects at different times by the teams themselves who can opt to work on or start up new initiatives, pulling together teams to explore new ideas. Their product through innovation is now part of everything from clothing (think Goretex™) to guitar strings, while also helping cardiac patients, firefighters and the military. According to founder Bill Gore, 'A lattice organisation is one that involves direct transactions, self-commitment, natural leadership and lacks assigned or assumed authority.' And it works. The company ticks each of the DRIVERS including providing clear recognition of the significance of every individual, using the natural formation of hierarchy to allow employees to understand both the system flow and their relative position within the system, without diminishing either their potential or self-worth.

Shifting towards a flatter hierarchy does have its problems. In April 2015, Dan Price, the CEO of Gravity Payments, brought in a minimum wage of $70K. This decision was inspired by a conversation with a friend who told him about Daniel Kahneman and Angus Deaton's paper that found that people's emotional wellbeing improves as their earnings rise, until their pay reaches about $75,000 a year. To partway fund the $1.8 million rise in the salary bill, with some employees doubling their wage, he dropped his own remuneration down to $70K. Dan became front-page news, with some media outlets placing him as the counter-inequality fairy and others assuming he had something to hide. This change, however, had its fallout. It rocked established individual significance for those whose salary was linked to their perception of their position within the organisation. Long-serving individuals quit because they were not able to square the shift in their perceived position which had previously been defined and cemented by a differential in earnings.

Another company that has sought to level the playing field of hierarchy is Zappos. In 2015, Tony Hsieh, CEO of shoe company Zappos, removed all management roles in the aim of becoming a Holacracy, a self-managed structure without management roles or job titles. Holacracy takes its name from the Greek word holos: a single, autonomous, self-sufficient unit that is, at the same time, dependent on a larger unit. It is akin to systems thinking, which was made famous by Peter Senge. He explored the inter-relationships and forces that shape the behaviour of the system – in this case the organisation. Those who felt uncomfortable in this new world were offered payment should they choose to leave; 210, 14% of them, walked, which included 7% of the managers.

All that said, whilst the fallout for both organisations was in the first instance painful, what remains are highly successful businesses following a new cultural and matrixed system of interaction and self-management. To understand the reasons a little more about why this self-sorting matrix is successful, I want to step back for a moment to evolutionary biology. An evolutionary biologist at Purdue University named William Muir wanted to understand chicken productivity[31] – an egg counting task! He created two groups of hens. One was simply your average flock and the other was the top-laying super hens flock. He studied these two groups for six generations. The first flock did well but in the super hen flock only three remained alive; the rest had been pecked to death by the others, hence the term pecking-order. Individual competition had been suppressed literally to death, which of course has the added consequence of no more eggs and, more profoundly, no more chickens!

MIT took this group productivity to their research teams. They brought in hundreds of volunteers, put them into groups and got them to solve complex problems. The groups that were most successful were not the ones with the highest IQ. The highest performing teams were those that were most socially sensitive to each other, showing the greatest degree of empathy and giving equal time to each other with no one voice being dominant, but equally there were no free-riders.[32] Zappos, W.L. Gore and Gravity all support this in their own way and reap the rewards as a consequence.

The crucial message is not that we should remove hierarchy but understand the difference between how much hierarchy is imposed or is self-formed. There is a place between dictatorship and anarchy that hears every individual's voice, provides a structure that supports a sense of a positive relative position, and values the significance of every person's contribution. The question is, are we brave enough to learn from the lessons learnt by Robert Sapolsky's baboons or William Muir's chickens?

What if...

Understanding how crucial social significance and our relative position is to us allows us as leaders to build this into our approach and decisions.

What if... we supported natural leadership and team formation? Leaving our teams to self-form is not about a corporate version of Escape from New York but an approach that trusts that the adults working for us, wanting to do a good job, will ultimately self-manage and form productive teams where everyone's contribution is understood and valued. We can support participative companies where titles are not required, enforced hours are outdated, holiday is unlimited and profit is shared by all. An adult environment, just think! Many companies are seeing the rewards from embracing this but it remains a large step for many organisations, although perhaps one worth taking a path towards?

What if... we structured reward on whole team output rather than individual ranking and scoring during performance reviews? Individual competition through scores on performance doors serves to divide and inject threat into the system as we clamber for position.

What if... we recognised the strengths and value delivered by every person? Ensuring the whole team understands the value and interdependency of everyone's contribution in relation to creating the final product, whatever that may be, is vital.

What if... we stop the talent tracks, the star players labels and the awards for the gifted and instead focus on the potential of all? Creating exclusive paths for certain individuals establishes skewed status and elitism and leaves everyone else out in the cold with a clear message that they are less worthy. That is not to say that effort and contribution above and beyond should not be recognised but perhaps instead of arbitrary scoring to pick out the top talent the team itself should be the ones to nominate.

What if... we leveraged the social capital in a culture of helpfulness and mutual respect rather than individualism? As we move into the fourth industrial age our need to collaborate is ever more crucial if we are to innovate and adapt. After all, companies don't have ideas, people do.

What if... we allowed a natural shift around leadership responsibility on different projects? Flexing the leadership allows not only continued development but also reforming of teams around strengths and experience.

CHAPTER 4
INCLUSION

'For firstly, the social instincts lead an animal to take pleasure in the society of his fellows, to feel a certain amount of sympathy with them, and to perform various services for them.'

Charles Darwin, *The Descent of Man*

The What...

Have you ever been excluded from a group, not invited to a party? Have you ever quietly and anxiously suspected that the clandestine conversation you saw between two friends or colleagues was about you? How did it feel? Nearly all of us would have felt the heartbreak of homesickness, many the pain of a divorce and the trauma of bereavement. Think of a team you belong/belonged to, be it your family, close group of friends, the place you go where 'everyone knows your name'. Put the scene in your mind's eye and tap into how you feel. What if I said you could have all the money you'd ever need but you'd never see another person again – would you accept the offer? What really makes us happy is our relationships.

When it comes down to it, humans are social creatures. Over our evolutionary journey, we have survived and thrived because we have worked together for mutual protection and support. We are far stronger together than on our own. Our ability to collaborate has allowed us to rise to the top of the evolutionary tree despite our relatively under-equipped physiques. We have no claws, no huge teeth, we can't run particularly fast and our young cannot fend for themselves for much of their early lives. It was only because another human being looked after our infant selves that we survived the first stage of our life's journey. Without the help of others, we would have perished.

From our brain's perspective exclusion is a direct threat to our survival. We instinctively know this. Think about it: throughout history exclusion through exiling or shunning has been used as punishment. At schools or in the home, teachers and parents are encouraged to use tactics such as 'time out' and the naughty step, which delivers the message of correction through exclusion. The need for belonging appears to have multiple and potent effects on emotional patterns and cognitive processes. A lack of attachments is linked to a variety of adverse effects on health, adjustment and wellbeing. The need (as opposed to a *want*) to belong is a powerful, fundamental and extremely pervasive human motivation.[33]

Sometimes we take it for granted and sometimes it can feel overwhelming, but the ability to relate to each other and manage multiple relationships is arguably the most complicated thing humans can do. It is a key reason for the size and complexity of our brain, particularly the cortex, the area of the brain that gives us, amongst other aspects, our ability for empathy, planning, decisions and language. Connecting to those around us is more complex than building the proverbial rocket, writing a symphony, or even the study of neuroscience! In an interview about his book *Born to Be Good,* Dacher Keltner, director of Berkeley Social Interaction Laboratory, recently said, 'Our mammalian and hominid evolution have crafted a species – us – with remarkable tendencies toward kindness, play, generosity, reverence and self-sacrifice, which are vital to the classic tasks of evolution: survival, gene replication and smooth functioning groups. These tendencies are felt in the wonderful realm of emotion – emotions such as compassion, gratitude, awe, embarrassment and mirth.' [34]

This sums up the quite remarkable and all-encompassing quality of our capacity for connection, alongside its significance for our surviving and thriving. Devoting resources to others, rather than indulging a materialist desire, brings about lasting wellbeing.[35]

To belong or not to belong

What would you say if I asked you to list your most painful memories – would you rate the death of a loved one or the betrayal of a best friend above or below a bike accident or broken arm? I'd suggest the former. The pain associated with a broken personal connection can feel disastrous and have more intense or protracted long-term repercussions, with the memory of the experience etching itself on to our brain's circuitry for the rest of our lives. When we later think about that experience again we risk reopening the wound and reliving the pain. I only have to ask you about not being invited to a party or an argument with a close friend and you can access those painful emotions, whereas if I'd asked you to recall the last time you knocked your elbow or bumped your head, assuming there was no significant trauma, you probably wouldn't be able to remember.

The survival advantage for connection is clear and biologically hardwired. We have developed aversive signals for the things we need, and that includes others. For example, hunger and thirst are aversive signals that trigger the motivation for action to find food and water. Likewise, the social pain of exclusion or a broken relationship is an aversive signal to find and connect to others or mend broken bonds. Social pain is present from birth; it keeps us living close to one another. Babies cry if they are separated from their caregiver who, in turn, will experience a sense of pain when they hear their babies cry. The cry is a motivational trigger, prompting the caregiver to go and attend to their baby.

Matthew Lieberman and Naomi Eisenburger of St Louis University, through their ground-breaking research, have shown that social pain is registered in the same location of the brain as physical pain. They argue that social pain is tantamount to real pain. It's why we refer to our 'broken heart' and why being left out literally hurts. Their research into reducing social pain through acetaminophen (a physical pain reliever) even showed that painkillers taken for a headache could help with heartache.[36] Social pain, say Lieberman and Eisenburger, should be categorised under the pain banner; this is not to say it is the same as a broken bone or arthritis, but that it is as tangible. And social pain isn't just a direct experience. Witnessing social rejection and exclusion of another also activates these pain receptors.[37]

To belong is as vital as food

In 1943, Abraham Maslow wrote *A Theory of Human Motivation* in which he described his theory of the hierarchy of human needs. It is most often depicted by a pyramidal diagram with the most fundamental or physical basics such as food and shelter at the bottom, on top of which other needs are stacked, ascending in priority from safety and security, love and belonging, self-esteem, and finally at the zenith of the pyramid you arrive at self-actualisation, which refers to reaching our potential through accomplishing desired goals.[38] Maslow's suggestion was that the most basic level of needs must be met before an individual can focus on the higher needs. In this book, I argue that the needs of human beings are not hierarchical but combinatory – that is, not mutually exclusive but overlapping and have equal importance when trying to fuse intrinsic motivation. This is why the DRIVERS are not depicted hierarchically but as a set of factors that all necessitate support for optimal performance and wellbeing. Love and belonging is as fundamental a need for our survival as is food and shelter.

The biology of belonging

John Bowlby, British psychoanalyst, first wrote about this in *Attachment Theory*: a study of how human beings respond when hurt by or separated from loved ones. From infancy, the seeking of another for care has a clear survival and evolutionary advantage, which tacitly indicates just why social pain is so strong a threat response. The brain is a social organ shaped by interactions and experiences with others. Bowlby says that infants need to form a strong relationship with at least one caregiver for successful emotional development – in particular, the ability to regulate their emotions. It is the pre-frontal cortex (PFC) of the brain – the social part – that enables such regulation and helps a child relate to others. During our earliest relationships, we build the neural circuitry we'll use throughout life to relate and connect to others, constructing implicit patterns and rules of attachments by 12 to 18 months. Our brains are not at full maturity when we are born and the pre-frontal cortex, which is virtually non-existent before birth, is stimulated for growth by hormones released through connection – most strongly by love. If love is compromised or early experiences are dysfunctional, more negative unconscious patterns can embed and detrimentally shape our perception of and responses to others thereafter. In some cases, this can be combated.

Through the natural phenomenon of neuroplasticity, the brain can establish new neural patterns of perception and interpretation to build healthier, more resilient ways of thinking and behaving. But the growth of the PFC is not automatic; rather it builds connections through the interaction it has over time. A baby that does not receive love is likely to block growth of vital brain areas. From one study of Romanian orphans who were severely neglected, deprived of any attachment, left in their cots all day with no human contact or affection, the disturbing results showed that some of the children had 'black holes' in the white matter of their brains associated with attention, emotion processing and general cognition[39] where these areas had failed to grow. A child who feels loved and thus secure can explore the world from a strong foundation. But one that has not had such attachment has a lesser ability to relate to others and has an increased risk of experiencing difficulty in later life, with a higher likelihood of developing mental health problems. This book will not attempt an exploration into these significant long-term effects, but it is important to cement the link between social connection and wellbeing, while also illustrating how the need for a secure base persists throughout our life, pushing us to seek the reward of connection to others and the survival benefits it brings. As Louis Cozolino quips: *'We are not the survival of the fittest; we are the survival of the nurtured.'* [40]

John Cacioppo, neuropsychologist at the University of Chicago, explains that whilst we like to see others and ourselves as individual autonomous beings we are in fact biologically wired to link together.

We rely on others as we grow and then eventually we become the ones to be relied upon. When studying the effects of loneliness, Cacioppo described the pain caused by loneliness as a warning system for trauma to our social being, which is necessary to help us survive and prosper. Loneliness, he explains, is on the rise. In the 1980s, studies showed that approximately 20% of Americans felt lonely at any given point in time. Today it is estimated that this number has doubled.

Loneliness is more lethal in relation to the odds of dying earlier than excessive alcohol consumption or obesity. A lack of connection alters behaviour and is related to greater resistance to blood flow through the cardiovascular system. Isolation places our brains into a social preservation mode. Brain imagining shows that the lonelier the brain, the more our capacity to take on board the views and feelings of another is reduced because we are more concerned with our preservation than concern for others. Our empathy switches off and the more isolated we feel, the lower our capacity to reach out for connection, which is both ironic and tragic. We become hypervigilant, which in turn increases our likelihood of having negative interactions since we are always looking for the next foe. Loneliness increases defensiveness, depressive symptoms and the stress hormone cortisol as the body prepares to guard against threats. It increases the fragmentation of sleep and so decreases the ability to defuse stressful energy, potentially making us more impulsively erratic.

Another important biological system involved with social connection is vagal tone, which is controlled by the vagus nerve, the main nerve in the rest and digestive system. It exerts a calming effect on many tissues throughout our body, able to modulate tone of voice, slow breathing and heart rate, and control the early stages of digestion in the stomach. Because of its location in the brain stem the vagus also regulates our facial expressions, synchronising them with our heart rate and the state of our gut, thereby playing a large role in our emotional and social lives. When in a relaxed state, our breathing and heart rate idle at a slower speed than their default rate. Here the vagus nerve applies a 'brake' as it controls heart rate variability. For minor stresses, the vagus releases the brake, increasing heart rate encouraging us to act. This is far more precise and gentle than having to evoke the metabolically expensive fight or flight mechanism every time.

Individuals with a high resting vagal tone tend to lead physically and mentally healthier lives.[41] One reason for this may be that high vagal tone individuals are better able to respond to environmental and social stressors and are able to elicit feelings of trust and affiliation from others, which in survival terms increases 'evolutionary fitness'.[42] In other words, we are motivated to connect because it gives us an advantage for survival; connecting feels good and does us good, so we seek to give and receive from our social network and in turn attract others to us to connect – a virtuous circle of connection. The same thing applies for our teams at work. The more we give to the pursuit of connecting, the greater emotional reward we receive. Neuroscientist Stephen Porges of the University of Illinois at Chicago has long argued that the vagus nerve is the nerve of compassion. Several studies have shown the link between high vagal tone and positive pro-social interaction. Barbara Fredrickson of the University of North Carolina led research that showed the link between higher vagal tone, greater experience of positive emotions, and boosted positive social connections. This upward spiral in turn supports physical health. The participants of her study attended a six-week 'loving-kindness-meditation' course where they learned how to cultivate positive feelings of kindness and goodwill to themselves and others. Another group was placed on a waiting list for the course. Those who had the learning were then asked for 61 consecutive days to report on their meditation activity, emotional experiences, and their social interactions within the last day. Their vagal tone was measured before and after the study. Those who entered the study with higher vagal tone than others showed steeper increases in positive emotions. For all participants, as their positive emotions rose so did their reported positive social connections and, as these connections rose, so did their vagal tone. In comparison, those who were on the waiting list showed virtually no change over the course of the study. Fredrickson said of the results, '*The daily moments of connection that people feel with others emerge as the tiny engines that drive the upward spiral between positivity and health.*'[43]

Life is good in the blue

In 2004, Dan Buettner, American explorer and author, teamed up with *National Geographic* and longevity experts to identify the places in the world where people live measurably longer. They identified five locations where individuals reached the age of 100 at rates ten times greater than in the United States.[44] In each of these locations, referred to as Blue Zones, teams of scientists examined the populations to determine lifestyle characteristics to explain the longevity. They published nine common characteristics. Three of these characteristics relate to a sense of belonging: belonging to a faith-based community; living close to and putting their families first; being part of strong social circles that support healthy behaviours. The Blue Zone Okinawans in Japan, for example, create 'moais' – groups of five friends that commit to each other for life. Whilst of course there is a genetic component to a long life, our lifestyle plays a huge part. We need to add social connection to the list of healthy pursuits.

Dunbar's number

The size of the group matters as well if we are to effectively manage relationships in a way that supports connection. There are several pieces of research that suggest between 150 and 230 is the maximum. The most cited is 150 (or more precisely 147.6, although I'm not sure what 0.6 of a person looks like) which came out of the work done by British anthropologist Robert Dunbar. Dunbar found a correlation between the average social size of a group and that of a primate's neocortex, and he used this to extrapolate the results to propose the limit of 150, now known as Dunbar's number.[45] Dunbar looked at surveys of tribe sizes and villages to test his hypothesis, including a Neolithic farming village, Huttertie settlements, as well as basic army unit sizes. These all supported his estimations.

Having led large teams and worked with organisations containing enormous numbers of employees, I feel the maximum number for a leader to support effectively is closer to the 100 mark. This is based on opinion and experience, and applying this knowledge worked well in one financial services organisation that managed a significant change programme across its 11,000 employees. Here the identified change leaders were given groups called 'communities' of no more than 100 individuals. Whilst there remained a central process, the dissemination of information, the support for behavioural change, and the emotional support was very effective because no one leader, each of whom had received specialist change management training, was overwhelmed. Each could comfortably manage all the relationships within their community. When a group is larger than 150 a sense of control starts to wane and more stringent rules appear. Policies start to become more formal, silos can start to form as we look to hold on to our tangible connection, and a sense of detachment creeps in. This is often one of the tipping points for growing businesses that find themselves losing touch with the 'family' feel and see the need for a more formulaic approach to keeping cohesion.

So What?

The hormone of trust is often deemed to be oxytocin, which is released through connection and touch. New research suggests that the vagal nerve is closely connected to receptor networks for this neurotransmitter. Oxytocin calms the amygdala and can trigger the pre-frontal cortex to grow fibres that carry something called gamma butyric acid or GABA, which can extinguish the fear response. In fact, studies have indicated that if we are just shown or asked to imagine the image of someone we love and with whom we feel safe our bodies release oxytocin. Our imagination is powerful, and the technique of bringing into one's mind's eye that individual who represents our secure base is a powerful antidote to threat.

Belonging and connecting to a group is neurologically rewarding. Oxytocin arouses a good sensation and strengthens our trust for others, positively impacting on our desire to collaborate. Building a sense of connection, belonging and inclusion is vital for developing a high-performing team. This might seem like an obvious statement, but in work environments where individualism and internal competition exists and/or is encouraged, conflict not connection is the outcome with an inevitable impact on performance and relationships. Similarly, as the technology allows more of us to work remotely or in geographically dispersed teams, the task of developing intimate connections becomes harder. It is the role of the leader to address such obstacles and support a strong team connection, and it takes new skills to do so.

A secure base

Just as children need a secure base, establishing a secure base within the workplace will support individuals to collaborate and innovate, venturing into new fields. George Kohlreiser, American clinical and organisational psychologist at IMD and hostage negotiator, has studied secure-base leadership, translating his expertise in leadership and experience in establishing bonds in a hostage negotiation into the workplace. He explains how a secure-base leader provides a sense of protection, safety and caring, alongside a source of inspiration and energy to explore, take risks and seek challenges.[46] How you are treated and the trust you perceive with the individual who leads you is critical for your perceived safety at work. Most people who quit their jobs leave their managers, not their organisations. Kohlreiser's research found that secure-base leaders remain calm, accept and value the individual, see the potential in the individual, listen and inquire, direct focus towards the positive, encourage risk taking, provide opportunities for stretch and challenges, and are accessible at all times.[47] The drive to care is a required leadership skill. Kohlreiser's work on 'secure base' details evidence suggesting that employee engagement is directly linked to how line managers treat them. A secure base helps you move forward and keeps you focused. It provides a brain-safe environment where employees are more likely to tap into their innovative talent (which is accessible in this brain state), naturally taking us to seek expansion through curiosity. Therefore, leaders who can create a secure base harness the energy and motivation of their team.[48]

We need to think socially

Being able to think socially and with empathy is the foundation upon which good leadership is built. Matthew Lieberman describes social thinking as being like a reflex. Its function is to prepare us to think about events in terms of the minds of those involved. Evolution has built a social neural network that helps us see the world socially; it enables us to manage the relationships we have and attain those we need. Lieberman uses the term 'information DJs' to describe the process by which we stop just consuming information and begin to share it with others. This is essential for establishing and creating collaborative teams and living well with one another. He reminds us that sociality is crucial to become smarter, happier and more productive. Leaders who can create and leverage the social networks of their teams will grow performance, creativity and collaboration. When we are really connected to our teammates we will work harder to support and contribute to the group. We tend also to strive to complement the different skills and strengths brought by everyone, which deepens the group's overall capability. In so many workplaces we undervalue our inherent social inclination and nourish only that parochial part of us honed on tasks and results. For leaders, being socially focused is equally as important as being results focused.

All change

We are wired to move away from threat. Change represents a threat to the brain because we naturally fear the unknown. Change is an organisational norm and yet over 75% of change fails to meet its long-term goals because it fails to take full account of the emotional impact. By focusing on building an environment where everyone feels they belong and is secure in their perception of attachments with their colleagues and leader, the natural resistance to change can be offset. We feel safe to explore the unknown and more comfortable if we know that whatever the change we'll be able to cope because of the support we have.

I have led and been a part of many large organisational changes, both nationally and internationally, and it was my experience of change that led me to research the field of intrinsic motivation. I wanted to understand the source of resistance, why the emotional impact is so strong, and how I could create an environment that smoothly supported rather than forced my teams through the change. In every change the starting point, once the leadership had made their decision, was to provide rational explanations for the need for change and the road map to achieve the goal. Information was spun to focus on the benefits through hundreds of PowerPoint presentations sent to managers to cascade to their teams. Managers, often those who are less experienced, feel caught between the turmoil of what the change means to them, the scaremongering of the regulation, the enforced script to deliver the messages, and the inevitable resistance of their teams. I was one of those young and inexperienced managers when I first led a large finance restructuring involving the closure of six offices across the UK and the set-up of the replacement shared services centre. I played my part to the letter, delivering the slides to the satellite offices, rehearsing the scripts, but never really letting individuals know what it meant for them as people. In the face of being told, the result, amongst other behaviours, for those involved is to seek the information they need.

I will talk more about this in the chapter about Reliability, but as employees talk, gossip and discuss they not only look to fill in the missing facts but also flock together, creating resistance groups. The phrase, 'this is business, it's not personal' is simply wrong. When you are on the receiving end of change it is deeply personal! What I have understood and now am able to apply is how to lead change that starts with the emotional reasoning, not the rational. Not only does this ensure that the starting place is the same as the brain's process, but it also saves a huge amount of time and expense. I often refer to this in terms of painting a windowsill. Without first preparing the wood, over time no amount of paint will stick, no matter how thickly it is spread. But if the wood is treated, sanded and filled then the paint takes moments to put on and it will last. Ignoring the emotional responses to change leaves the paint peeling off.

Connection

Studies overwhelmingly display how social connection is one of the best predictors of happiness and wellbeing. Yet in today's modern world we find ourselves more isolated from our families, friends and potential connections as we move away or travel for work and manage the pressures of the work itself. Pursuing financial reward or career advancement can be at the expense of our social connection, decreasing our happiness. Is the life you are leading worth the price you are paying for it? Isolation for teams is a real business issue. Technological developments enable us to work anywhere, at any time (although for many this is a double-edged sword: anywhere anytime is not all the time!), but being less reliant on the office with the benefits it brings also means we can find ourselves distanced from those we work with and with whom we need to collaborate.

And it's not just in the workplace. Studies carried out on adolescents appear to be showing the problems that connecting with others in the main via social media is changing our brain's capability to connect with others when we are physically with them. The neuroscientist Baroness Susan Greenfield is leading the debate on this subject, asking governments to consider what she sees as great a threat to humanity as climate change. She argues that social media is affecting our sense of identity and ability to empathise. Let's think about this for a moment. Our brains are beautifully designed to adapt and shape their neural connections in part based on our environment and what we practise. If the main source of social interaction is formed online, using words that only represent around 10% of our social impact, then we are not rehearsing all the visual cues of communication and connection. 'If we don't use it, we lose it' is the view of neuroscientists when it comes to wiring the brain. So, will this mean we will deplete our ability to relate to others except via a screen? What does this mean for human connection, businesses and relationships? I don't think this is yet clear, but I understand Baroness Greenfield's call to at least discuss the possible impact, and whilst a great deal more research is required to understand the effects of social media, is it not better to open our eyes now?

With connection being a critical performance factor, leaders need to be highly vigilant of the isolation potential and actively work to establish and build connection – which is not an easy task if many teams collaborate across time zones and geographies. Studies, particularly on the military, show that cohesion in a group around a shared goal, also known as task cohesion, has a greater influence on performance than how well and often we get on with each other socially (social cohesion). After reviewing military and civilian studies of cohesion, Professor Robert MacCoun pointed out that *when social cohesion is too high, deleterious consequences can result, including excessive socialising, group-think (the failure of a highly cohesive group to engage in effective decision-making processes), insubordination, and mutiny*[49] – not so good in a business setting! And yet we often approach the need to create cohesion at work with team-bonding sessions and enforced socialising – something I'm sure most of us have had the dubious pleasure of attending. It's not that taking time away from the office as a group is a bad thing – in fact, quite the opposite. More importance, however, should be placed on shared purpose and tasks than social bonding to knit the team together. In terms of survival it's not how much I like my teammate but our joint desire to attain our goals that cements our relationship. I have spoken about the importance of purpose, meaning and direction, so it's not surprising that task cohesion fits the bill when establishing belonging within a group. The reward from the support I get from those around me working towards a shared and commonly desired outcome is hugely motivating.

Are you in or out?

On the darker side of this topic, we find silos, group-think and unhealthy competition between teams. This is where individual agendas are pursued, outsiders are actively pushed away and risk grows. A little in-house competition can provide a sense of excitement and motivation, but this can be quickly replaced with an almost tribal lockdown between teams. Work may be organised rationally between teams in terms of work types and specialisms, which for the most part is efficient but only effective if those departments/teams understand and value the dynamics of the workflow between them and their mutual interdependencies. Because of our need to belong, to identify with a group, we can unintentionally erect invisible barriers that block out those not in the 'in-group', which is determined by the team's specialism or project. Those in the 'out-group' are considered 'not good enough', somehow inferior, and while niceties will be passed between those out and those in, each 'in-group' member ultimately seeks the safety of the team and, as such, the group retreats into itself. I've seen this happen time and time again. The sales team cursing procurement, client-facing teams criticising finance and so on. It blocks the system and stifles ideas and development. Silos can appear on the same floor or with teams that sit within a yard of each other. When physical structures are there such as floors, walls, or even just a table, the split can often be emphasised.

Have you ever sent an email to the person who sits a few yards from you rather than getting up and speaking to them? I worked with a group of IT support professionals during a study to examine why the department was floundering and the engagement scores were so low. During the usual introductions, the following conversation happened:

> *'Hi, I'm Jane. I'm a system analyst working in xx department.'*
> *'Oh, are you Jane Thompson?'*
> *'Yep.'*
> *'I'm John, John Simons.'*
> *'Gosh, hi, good to finally meet you, we must email every day with those data issues.'*
> *'Whereabouts are you?'*
> *'Just by the coffee machine on this floor – you?'*
> *'What, the one by the lifts?'*
> *'Yep.'*
> *'So am I. You're not on the bank of desks literally next to it are you?'*
> *'Yes.'*
> *'Ha, I'm on the bank just after that, behind the pillar. After all this time we sit just a few metres apart.'*

The key to changing this is to focus on the social reward of work. We are social creatures first, and we need others to fulfil our individual and collective potential. Connecting teams with a common purpose and goal is a sure-fire way of bringing two factions together.

*'The assumption that productivity is about smart people
working on their own has been masking the fact that
individual intelligence may only be optimised when it is
enhanced through social connections to others in the group.'* [50]
Matthew Lieberman

Silos reduce idea generation. When we work with like-minded individuals who do the similar things we do, we decrease our field of view and shrink our capacity to link, collaborate and create new thinking. Diversity and inclusion (D&I) is a function established in organisations over the past 15 years. The work done has been important to lower and break demographic barriers to employment entry and promotion. But D&I is still most often seen as a necessary requirement to tick the regulatory boxes, even an annoyance rather than a strategically critical area focused on optimal performance. Innovation happens when individuals continually bring different experiences, backgrounds, knowledge and perspectives. Once a team has been established, the effect of any demographic diversity can diminish as thinking and working around the same tasks and subject overtakes. This can lead to group-think.

Group-think is a term coined by Irving Janis in the early 1970s. [51] It reduces the capacity to look at challenges from different perspectives, often leading to faulty decisions due to the pressures coming from the perceived social norms of the group. Groups tend to ignore alternatives, dismiss other 'out-group' ideas, and can become increasingly irrational as they circle around the syndrome of 'this is how we do it here' or 'that won't work here'. Groups where everyone's background is similar are particularly and unsurprisingly vulnerable to group-think. Janis studied examples of group-think 'fiascos', including the US failure to anticipate the attack on Pearl Harbour, the escalation of the Vietnam War, and decisions made by the Bush administration around pre-emptive use of military force against terrorists in Iraq that rushed the

US into war. Group-think adversely affects business decisions because it supports a collective bias that, when processing information, will lead to individuals or the group selecting only information that confirms or aligns with the entrenched ways of thinking. It also hinders the ability to appraise a situation objectively and search for alternatives when something goes wrong. Psychologists also refer to this type of decision error as confirmation bias or sometimes called 'myside' bias. Individuals who are subject to group-think select information that supports their existing views and can lead to an overconfidence in, and strengthening of, opinion despite contrary evidence. Janis listed eight symptoms of group-think:

1. Illusion of invulnerability – Creates excessive optimism that encourages taking extreme risks.
2. Collective rationalisation – Members discount warnings and do not reconsider their assumptions.
3. Belief in inherent morality – Members believe in the rightness of their cause and therefore ignore the ethical or moral consequences of their decisions.
4. Stereotyped views of out-groups – Negative views of 'enemy' make effective responses to conflict seem unnecessary.
5. Direct pressure on dissenters – Members are under pressure not to express arguments against any of the group's views.
6. Self-censorship – Doubts and deviations from the perceived group consensus are not expressed.
7. Illusion of unanimity – The majority view and judgments are assumed to be unanimous.
8. Self-appointed 'mind-guards' – Members protect the group and the leader from information that is problematic or contradictory to the group's cohesiveness, view and/or decisions.

When I first read this list, my thoughts went to the behaviour of the banks in the lead-up to, during, and since the global financial crash of the early 21st century. A lot of work has been done around behavioural economics in assessing why individuals and groups made such disastrous decisions with the vital funds in their care, and certainly this blind-sided thinking would have played a large part.

Let's talk

It is social capital that drives business and needs focus and attention to nurture and build. Businesses run on trusted relationships and their conversations. Good conversations reduce error rate, stimulate innovation, and speed up the process of ideas. As we move deeper into the innovation economy and onward to the fourth industrial age of digitalisation, and the boundaries of human knowledge extend and grow ever more complex, we need to capitalise on working together to answer questions the future will pose. But what is the best way to support collaboration that connects individuals to the group and taps into the associated neurological rewards? One possible way is through good old brainstorming.

Alex Osborn, a partner in the advertising agency BBDO, published a book, *Your Creative Power*, in the late 1940s, to share his creative secrets. One of the keys to his creative success, he wrote, was brainstorming and so the management tool was born. He outlined the need for 'free-wheeling' associations, the absence of judgment, negative feedback or criticism of any idea. A space for every person to contribute. Brainstorming was first empirically tested by Yale University in 1958. The same puzzles were given to 12 different groups and were also given to an equal number of individuals working on their own. Surprisingly, those working on their own came up with approximately twice the number of possible solutions that when reviewed separately were said to be 'feasible' and 'effective'. A number of studies have come to the same conclusion, suggesting that brainstorming actually diminishes the creativity of the individual when working within a group. All is not lost, however, because studies done by Charlan Nemeth in 2004[52] found that Osborn's rule, one of the basic premises of brainstorming technique of no criticism was the issue. Her study calls this premise into question in that the encouragement to debate and even criticise not only does not inhibit idea generation, it appears to enhance it even more than the traditional brainstorming instructions. She found that when debate was introduced creativity was sparked, something she labelled as the 'debate condition'. From my standpoint, I would add a further element to this form of collaboration. Debate is healthy, but participants must feel safe to offer ideas and have the skills to present objective critique so that it doesn't place others' brains in a threat state. I explore the reward we get from both being genuinely heard within our group in the chapter on Relative Position, but for now it suffices to say that judgmental and subjective criticism will undermine and demotivate, shutting down innovation.

Bringing together individuals from across different specialisms rather than just tackling a problem within a team can add greater depth and perspective. Steve Jobs, often seen as the king of innovation, used architecture to force interactions across his organisation. As he planned the Pixar headquarters, he designed an atrium that 'promoted encounters and unplanned collaborations'. He put meeting rooms, mailboxes, the coffee bar, and even the only set of toilets into the centre of the building (he was later forced to compromise on this and install a second pair of bathrooms). He was quoted as saying, 'Everyone has to run into each other, creating a spatial arrangement that encouraged innovation and the magic sparked by serendipity.' He believed that the best meetings happen by chance, be they from bumping into someone in the park, hallway or even the bathroom! This new design created a shared hub, bringing together the organisation's varied disciplines that had originally been separated in different buildings. He created a space where animators could talk to sound engineers and storyboarders, a place that leveraged our instinct to work together, tapping into the biological reward of collaboration. The current president of Pixar, Ed Catmull, reinforces the focus on connection and relationships for innovation. He refers to the organisation as 'a community in the true sense of the word... in filmmaking and many other kinds of complex product development, creativity involves a large number of people from different disciplines working effectively together to solve a great many problems.' [53]

What if...

So, I hope that I have given you enough to convince you of the imperative for inclusion. To look about you and know you belong, are supported and that someone always has your back. The amount of research and studies on this subject is vast and I could devote the whole book to it, but I obviously won't because there is much more to say on the other DRIVERS. But what can and should we do to create the environment of true inclusion?

What if... we can connect individuals through a shared goal or task bringing them together from different teams, disciplines and backgrounds – embracing difference? When Jobs brought design teams from the animation company Pixar into the failing technology company Apple, the iPhone and all things associated was the result.

What if... we think of our businesses not as transactional units but as a society formed of interdependent communities that identify and work together to build the whole? The lifeline is conversation and positive interaction through which ideas flow, tasks are completed and trust is established. All of us are smarter than any one of us and whilst a small level of competition is good fun, watch out for targets, performance measures, processes and financial incentives that drive individualism. When we start to focus only on ourselves the result is damage to the community and ultimately to the business. Let's reward behaviours that promote collaboration and giving back to the team.

What if... we apply Dunbar's number to never overcrowd or stifle the community links, mitigating the risk of silos forming?

What if... leaders worked to establish the secure base from which each member of the team can take risks to create and feel safe to question?

What if... we approached innovation by asking individuals to first work on a challenge alone and then bring their thoughts to the team to be deliberated through safe debate that gives space for every person to be heard whilst allowing critique and opinion to mould the ideas? We need to remain aware of and challenge group-think and echo chambers.

What if... we consciously share the good times? Recognise the team's strengths and potential. Notice and reflect on the effort and achievements, not an outweighed focus on error, weaknesses and what's not yet been achieved. Assume first that the intention was to succeed and if things don't go as planned use it to learn and demonstrate that you have their back.

What if... we focused on developing managers and leaders to strengthen their skills for conversation and ability to deepen the sense of inclusion for all, focusing on the relationships and what really builds and nurtures them? What if we provide leaders the knowledge to be able to recognise the aversive behavioural signals of exclusion, and instead of reacting with annoyance or distance, to know how to act to close the rift?

CHAPTER 5
VOICE AND CHOICE

'Time is the coin of life. It is the only coin you have and only you can determine how it will be spent. Be careful lest you let other people spend it for you.'

Carl Sandburg

'Freedom is realising you have a choice.'

T F Hodge

The What...

Ever felt like there is just too much to do: the mounting housework, the tile that's fallen off and needs repairing, the play date you owe...? And, on top of these nagging concerns there are the fast-approaching work deadlines, the meeting you need to present at, the never-ending conveyor belt of emails jamming your inbox... Does any of this resonate? How does it make you feel? How do you behave? A sense of uncontrollability, feeling overwhelmed, and an increased tendency towards procrastination are common responses. They certainly are for me, usually leading to bubbling frustration from uncontrollable inundation eventually boiling over as I shout at my husband for being so thoughtless as to stand in the wrong place! Add to this scene being micromanaged at work by a manager who is intent on controlling every aspect of your work. And, to make things yet worse, compound these anxieties with worries about not paying as much attention as you want or know is necessary to your family, friends, exercise and hobbies – the good old work-life balance conundrum. A term I dislike, mind you, as it assumes that work and life are distinct entities, which they are not. When I last looked, my life included work and I haven't yet learned to split myself in two. That said, the ever-mounting challenge of integrating and being able to prioritise all the important aspects of our lives remains.

Now imagine another situation. You are accused of something you didn't do. You are arrested and imprisoned. No one listens to your pleas of innocence. What's going through your mind now? How do you feel?

I fully appreciate this last example is extreme by way of demonstration but it helps explain how, as our sense of voice and control diminishes, so does our perception of choice and autonomy. To our brains, this represents danger. If the neurological interpretation of events is that we have a lack of choice and control, then it follows that our safety has been placed in the hands of others and the outside world. I have lost count of the people with whom I've worked who have fallen into a world where they feel they have little say in their worlds. Some feel subservient to the pay packet, which provides them with purchasing power at the price of all-consuming work (which is both actual and, of their own thoughts, telling them to be present and online at all times) whilst others are shackled to work all hours to simply make ends meet. Whether it is the blackberry, the controlling boss, finances, workload, or simply our own thoughts, a lack of choice and control is deeply threatening and leaves us feeling downtrodden, exhausted and ineffective.

In his book *Man's Search for Meaning*, psychiatrist and neurologist Victor Frankl (1905-1997) details his ordeal as a WWII concentration camp prisoner at Auschwitz. He noted that those who survived longest in the camp were not those who were physically strong but those who retained a sense of control over their environment. He wrote of his observation: '*We who lived in concentration camps can remember the men who walked through the huts comforting others, giving away their last piece of bread. They may have been few in number, but they offer sufficient proof that everything can be taken from a man but one thing: the last of human freedoms – to choose one's own attitude in any given set of circumstances – to choose one's own way.*'

The subject of choice and control has been widely debated across the fields of psychology and philosophy. One hotly debated subject within neurophilosophy is the area of free will. Do we really have complete freedom of choice when in fact, as I've written about, it's our unconscious mid-brain that is really in charge, determining our behaviour based on the filing cabinet's categorisation of events? Much of the neurophilosophical research has looked at decision making and how our non-conscious mid-brain fires before our conscious self. One of the most famous experiments was carried out by Benjamin Libet who, in the 1970s, studied human consciousness and involved participants moving a finger. Whilst monitoring brain activity, Libet and his team would ask individuals to carry out some simple movements within a specified time, such as flexing their finger or pressing a button. They were also asked to mark on an oscilloscope timer the point at which they had the thought or urge to make the movement. Libet also recorded the point at which the actual movement was made. The results showed that brain activity involved in the action was around 500 milliseconds before the 'urge' to act and 700 milliseconds before the actual movement. Libet concluded that the build-up of electrical activity related to movement preceded both conscious awareness and final action. He called this Bereitschafts potential or readiness potential.

So, what? Well, we all like to think we have complete agency over our actions and that our fully conscious self forms the decisions we make. Yet Libet's study problematises this notion, calling our sense of agency into question and even going as far as to say that free will does not play any part in our actions, but – and this is the bit that makes the most sense to me – what agency we do possess is best described as a free *won't* than a free *will*. As we have explored, the mid-brain is managing our survival, moving us away from threat and towards reward and safety based on its interpretation of events. It is highly efficient at doing so but not, in today's world, necessarily right or helpful. Our conscious and rational neo-cortex provides not the initial interpretative analysis or the associated primary response (that is the job of the mid-brain which has neurological primacy, in other words it is always first up), but it does have the capability to review, adjust and veto. This freedom to choose our response to events forms the basis of resilience and helps us restrain our actions, which without 'free won't' would be purely impulsive. This power of veto over the mid-brain is demonstrated through those with damage to certain areas of the pre-frontal cortex and fall foul of the mid-brain's choices.

Probably the most famous example of this is the case of Phineas Gage who in 1848, whilst working as a railroad construction foreman, unbelievably survived an accident that drove a tamping iron (a large iron rod) straight through his skull, destroying most of his left pre-frontal lobe. Before the accident, Gage was described as hardworking, responsible, efficient and a 'great favourite' with the men. After, his behaviour was described in the literature as *'fitful, irreverent, indulging at times in the grossest profanity (which was not previously his custom), manifesting but little deference for his fellows, impatient of restraint or advice when it conflicts with his desires, at times pertinaciously obstinate, yet capricious and vacillating, devising many plans of future operations, which are no sooner arranged than they are abandoned in turn for others appearing more feasible.'*

Most interesting is the sentence about him stating that *'the equilibrium or balance, so to speak, between his intellectual faculties and animal propensities, seems to have been destroyed.'*

Having been stripped of the freedom to override its impulses, Gage became subject to his mid-brain's will. The good news, however, is that we can learn to increase our free won't. There are cognitive techniques we can use to deepen the regulation of the mid-brain and choose our final action and attitude. Is this then free will? I'll leave you to decide and debate. The crucial takeaway from this initial examination of choice is its relationship to our work. As we build our 'veto response' so too do we improve our decision making, deepening the partnership between our mid-brain and our rational self. We need both our experience held with our files and our capacity for objective questioning to work together as we assess strategy and direction. Too much of either can reduce our decision potential, but this collaboration of the emotional and the rational requires trust.

This chapter will look at choice, control and autonomy in relation to our brain's interpretation – our perception. As with the other

DRIVERS, if our voice and choice is perceived to be supported it will deliver trust and reward, leading to engagement and higher performance. But if it is perceived as quashed, even if, in reality, we remain free to choose another course, this will trigger a threat state impacting negatively on performance. Even if you are unable to control others or events, the ability to choose your attitude and actions remains in your control. As the Greek philosopher Epictetus is quoted as saying, 'It's not what happens to you, but how you react to it that matters.' Or in the words of Henry Ford, who for me sums it up best, 'Whether you think you can or you think you can't – you're right.'

So What?

It's all a perception of choice

In the workplace, providing an environment of perceived choice, autonomy and control is a necessary function for high-performing teams. When autonomously functioning, people are more deeply engaged and productive. Think about a recent change at work, or in fact any change. How often did you hear or use phrases like: 'they told us' or 'it's come from above', and variations on a theme? Who 'they' are is immaterial, although it can be assumed to be at an undefined leadership level. What matters is what's behind the words – what is not said. The words 'they told us' is a veil for 'I've not been asked… I've not been given a choice'. You may at this point be thinking that it's not always possible to give choice and hand over control, particularly through change, and I'd agree to a certain extent. But there are always ways of supporting a sense of control and choice. I recently worked with a company looking to bring in a more flexible approach to work within a field-based operational team. The leadership found it hard to understand how they could implement flexibility alongside effectively managing logistics such as who had the vans if a role was shared or part-time. Instead of moving away and doing nothing, labelling it as too hard a problem, the leadership handed the challenge over to the field workers who, as it happened, solved the problem. Subsequently they reported a feeling of influence, control and greater engagement, which fed through into the ownership of the change itself.

Our perception of choice and control and its importance to our thriving has been shown in many studies. Perceived control plays an important part in maintaining a healthy lifestyle and can even be a factor to our living longer. The Max Planck Institute for Human Development in Berlin has carried out a 16-year study examining perceived control in over 3,000 participants. Their statistical results showed the level of perceived control predicted long-term mortality risks independent of demographic factors.[54] The researchers have drawn the conclusion that seeing life as controllable and predictable helps to regulate and protect against negative emotions.

Another study (and a favourite of mine) is Ellen Langer and Judith Rodin's 1975 research conducted at Arden House,[55] a nursing home in Connecticut. They wanted to understand the effects of enhanced personal influence on the wellbeing of elderly residents who were living virtually choice-free as the nursing home ensured every care was attended to. Arden house was a well-run large home with approximately 300 residents at the time. Langer and Rodin chose two floors to study, the second and the fourth, because of the similarity in the residents' physical and psychological health, length of stay and prior socio-economic status. Baseline health measurements were taken of the residents within the study and, whilst the subjects could not be randomly assigned to the experimental treatments, the treatments were randomly assigned between the two floors, giving rise to two groups: 1) The Responsibility-induced group and 2) The Comparison group.

First the groups were given a talk by a member of the nursing team to introduce the study. Group 1 were told that they had influence over many things at the home, like how they wanted their rooms arranged, when they wanted visitors, how to spend their time, that they were at liberty to offer up complaints and suggestions for change. In other words, 'it is your life and you can make of it whatever you want'. This group were also told that a film would be shown two nights a week and they had the choice to attend or not. Finally, they were given the option to choose a plant from a variety on offer and were told that it was their responsibility to care for the plant, as they wished. The comparison group were told that that their rooms had been laid out for them as nicely as the staff could do them, that a film would be shown twice a week and they would be told which day they were scheduled to see it, and, just like the other group, they'd be given a plant as a gift from Arden house, but their plants would be cared for by the nursing staff. The major difference between these two groups is the emphasis on their sense of influence, choice and control. The responsibility-induced group had a level of control over their environment while being in the care of staff, whereas the comparison group had minimal responsibility for themselves. There was, however, no difference in the amount of attention paid to the two groups.

The results were astonishing and went beyond Langer and Rodin's expectations. In 93% of the responsibility group, providing them with a greater sense of control showed improvements in activity and self-reported happiness in as short a period as three weeks of the experiment, versus 71% of the comparison group, who were rated as more debilitated in the same period. More importantly, however, when Langer and Rodin returned to the home 18 months later they found that twice as many of the comparison group had died in relation to the responsibility group. The idea that just having a plant to look after or choosing when you want to see a film can extend life is extraordinary, almost unbelievable, but the experiment has been repeated since and yielded the same results. Langer went on to study how giving greater control to hospitalised patients had a positive effect on their medication levels. Choice and a sense of control have a ripple effect. Greater choice helps keep self-esteem intact, deepens the motivation to connect to others and take part, and support a sense of purpose.

Around the same time another study was being carried out within the field of control and choice, albeit using unethical methodology that would not be used today. Martin Seligman used dogs to demonstrate learnt helplessness.[56] In his experiment one dog would learn to escape an electric shock by jumping over a box, while another would receive random electric shocks irrespective of anything it tried to do. The second dog learned that it had no control over the event, and two thirds of these dogs gave up trying even when a clear route to escape was provided, remaining helpless to their situation. Later Seligman was able to connect this sense of helplessness to symptoms of depression in humans. When we perceive we have no choice, that we are helpless and the situation is hopeless, we spiral downward towards defeat. In the analysis of prisoner of war camps by Bruno Bettelheim,[57] survival *'depended on one's ability to arrange to preserve some areas of independent action, to keep control of some important aspects of one's life despite an environment that seemed overwhelming and total.'*

Probably one of the most famous psychologists in this area is Julian Rotter. He established and tested his theory of the 'locus of control' in 1954 and it has withstood the test of time. One's locus of control relates to how you believe things will turn out based on the extent to which you believe you have control over the events affecting you. He described this control as either internal or external. Those with an internal locus of control see that outcomes are influenced by their actions, in other words by internal factors such as effort, strengths and skills, whereas those with an external locus of control will put future results down to external factors such as others, luck, fate or chance, all of which place any perception of personal control out of reach. Rotter's theory shows us that it's our attitude and sense of influence over what we *realistically* can control that supports our success. Those higher on the scale of internal locus of control are seen to have higher job satisfaction and performance. Your sense of internal or external locus of control can change depending on the situation. We have all felt in control in one part of our lives where we know what is expected of us and we have the skills to match, while in other parts we feel unsure of what to do. Those with an internal locus of control are more likely to be proactive in the latter position and less likely to play 'victim' to the situation, seeking solutions, pulling on strengths, and finding ways of moving forward.

Ask don't tell

Too many well-intentioned changes and projects fail because people feel controlled rather than motivated by a sense of choice. When we perceive things are 'have to do' the brain interprets a punishment and we look to resist, avoid and even sabotage in our effort to defend. One remedy for this is in the question itself, which positions the task and can trigger what psychologists call reactance: our response to threats to our autonomy. The neural mechanisms underlying the way we assess the consequences of choices differ depending on whether we are told what to do or are able to exercise our volition.[58] In a meta-analysis of 42 studies involving over 22,000 participants, the conclusion showed that by simply adding the phrase 'but you are free to accept or refuse' doubled the likelihood of people saying yes to charitable donations and filling in voluntary surveys, because choice was extended.[59] Workplaces are not prisons intentionally set up to punish through the removal of choice, they are environments where every individual can remain autonomous, whether that be through how they approach work or in making the choice to stay or leave. It is asking, not telling, that pays dividends. During periods of change – an inevitable factor of organisational life – giving control and choice wherever possible, no matter how small, will smooth the path and build trust and engagement.

The good old work-life balance juggling act

We face what seems like the ever-mounting challenge of integrating the most important parts of our lives with work. I've mentioned before my dislike of the term work-life balance which, alongside flexible working, now carries many negative connotations. We take our whole selves wherever we go, work and life. The research into what's termed the work-life conflict shows us that the spillover from a lack of control in either of these realms directly and negatively affects the other.[60] Researchers have found that with an increased amount of negative spillover from work to family, the likelihood of reporting stress within the family increased by 74%, and with an increased amount of negative spillover from family to work the likelihood to report stress felt at work increased by 47%.[61]

The term work-life balance was first coined in the 1970s in the UK to describe the time spent between work and personal life. The first usage in the USA came in 1986, articulating growing concerns about the number of hours spent at work to the detriment of life outside of work. Much has been done on the political and employee relations front to try to address this challenge through broadening the right to request flexible working, but organisations and individuals still struggle with both the concept and the practical implementation. The problem runs deeper than simply updating HR flexible working policies. Flexible working is not just about one demographic of the workforce nor is it just about a formal change to contractual hours. In fact, I'd argue that in many corporate environments part-time is currently merely a reduction in pay, not workload or hours. Flexibility is, just as the word describes, an approach to work that supports choice and autonomy, affording a sense of control to the individual to integrate all the aspects of their lives, including work. Technology has given us the ability to work anywhere and at any time, but while this gives us a fantastic advantage to be autonomous, the opposite has become the reality. We are 'always on', always working or feeling unnecessarily guilty for not working, compounding the sense of lack of control and choice to balance life. It is not the volume of work we face that causes the deepest distress but our perception of the control we have to deal with it. Job control, including over tasks and pace of work, increases job and leisure satisfaction.[62] Organisations still routinely define contractual hours as 9 to 5 even though so many of their employees will work many more hours because they sense the culture demands it, afraid to leave earlier than others because of a worry that they will be perceived as less committed. Hot-desking, home working, job-share or any of the many approaches taken to implement flexible working only scratch the surface when it comes to supporting optimal performance. The key is mindset not policy.

When organisations first announce that they are looking to improve their flexible/agile/smart working (pick an adjective!) the resistance usually comes first from line management and above. If I had a pound for every time I've heard 'If we offer flexible working it will open the flood gates' or 'If they are working from home how will I know they are working?' When I hear these phrases or similar it tells me that the manager is feeling a threat to their own sense of control. Their behavioural response to this perceived threat might be a greater level of micro-managing to recover control, which in turn demotivates the team. Stanford neuroscientist Robert Sapolsky showed that when dominant monkeys are exposed to uncontrollable stressors they take to biting subordinates, which in turn lowers their cortisol (stress hormone) levels. I've often wondered if this could somewhat explain micro-managerial dominant behaviour. The more we shout and dictate, the more control we think we have.

Of course, micro-managing and being 'bossy' has the opposite effect: the more one tries to control others, the more threat is placed into the system, the more the performance of those being bossed is reduced, the more the boss needs to boss, and so on into the proverbial vicious cycle. In addition to individual managerial responses, at an organisational level those making the decisions often create a set of rules around flexibility that are paradoxically aimed at controlling access to freedom and choice. You may only work at home once a week; flexible hours must be carried out within certain periods or other diametric limitations to autonomy. Flexible working becomes exactly the opposite: the freedom is shackled in bureaucracy and power play. Rules often put in place to mitigate the risk of abuse to the system start from a premise of distrust. We need to let go of the controls and trust that we have the right people in the right jobs wanting to do a good job. So, in the words of Jack Welch, former CEO of GE, 'Give them the tools to do the job then get out of their way.'

I've worked with many organisations to dispel the myths and beliefs about flexible working and work-life balance. Redefining flexibility as choice and autonomy means loosening the reins. It might seem contradictory to take your foot off the pedal to go faster, but as practical steps are implemented leaders soon realise the positive results and re-establish their own sense of control. One study has shown this over and above all others: the 'Results Only Work Environment' (ROWE) first researched and embedded by two HR managers, Jody Thompson and Cali Ressler of the US company BestBuy. Their concept was simple: 'We'll measure only your results, we don't care about where you work, what time you work; there are no fixed schedules, just get your work done.' There are no contractual hours and no set holiday days, which for most companies would seem like a step too far, but the results from their ongoing work are unmistakable. Thompson and Ressler realised early on that what people were really looking for was greater control and autonomy. Their definition for ROWE, which they proposed to an initially terrified leadership, was that 'each person is free to do whatever they want, whenever they want, as long as the work gets done.' They were told that this was ridiculous, that they couldn't simply trust people to work. In fact, one person said that this could bring down the global economy!

When Phyllis Moen studied ROWE,[63] she took 325 employees who had spent six months in ROWE and a control group of 334 employees who continued with their normal work arrangements. The ROWE participants could freely determine when, where and how they worked. The employees could decide if they wanted to work from home, start the day at 11am, miss meetings (so long as a team member covered for them), or make any other personal accommodations as they saw fit. After six months, the employees who participated in ROWE reported reduced work-family conflict and a better sense of control of their time, and they were getting a full hour of extra sleep each night. The employees were less likely to leave their jobs, resulting in reduced turnover. They were even more likely to go and see a doctor if they needed to. And topping all this off, the job got done.

Without the stress of perceived uncontrollability, alongside the reward from autonomy, our brains are back online, regaining their capacity for efficiency and innovation while also reaping the health benefits. Yet to implement such a radical change to the workplace remains out of reach for most. An expectation of people running amok when given the privilege of working as they wish leaves many tasked with leadership cold. The crux here, as with all the DRIVERS, is trust. Choice, control and autonomy build trust, engagement and loyalty. Those that abuse the system are likely to abuse the system with or without autonomy and for reasons that will relate to the individual case and/or other DRIVERS being quashed. Employing adults means treating them as such, which includes choice returned in kind as accountability.

What is the right choice?

Now on to another common cause of underperformance: promotion. Have you heard of the term 'promoted to the level of incompetence'? Pretty damning in its appraisal of the situation, but so often, particularly when promoted to leadership, an individual's performance can drop significantly after promotion. This is somewhat ironic, considering promotions are most likely based on past high performance. There is often an assumption that a capable person will continue to be capable. This would be true if they had all the knowledge and skills, but those skills are often miles away from the roles they had before. Technical brilliance does not automatically make for a brilliant leader; the two jobs carry different requirements. The phenomenon is termed the 'Peter Principle', a concept put forward by Laurence Peter who went so far as to say that, 'In time, every post tends to be occupied by an employee who is incompetent to carry out its duties.' [64] Quite amusing if you think about it in terms of who is actually running our companies. But on a more serious note, being put in a role without the skills leaves us feeling out of control, exacerbating the issue because the stress we are placed under depletes our capacity and energy to perform or try to find a solution. A choice to seek out training or to say that we are struggling is of course an option, but faced with a culture that doesn't appear to encourage this or our own thoughts about how we may be perceived to be failing can hamper our attempts to progress, leaving individuals floundering.

This chapter, as the title suggests, is about having our voice heard and our choice respected in what and how we do things. But in a world where work has become so consuming, even when we are afforded choice we sometimes don't know how to make the right one or even see the paths available to us. As the media rubs our noses in the celebrity super-heroes juggling glittering careers with family commitments, owning beautiful homes, with toned bodies and successful hobbies thrown in, how do we ensure we match up? People struggling to integrate priorities in and out of work have often asked me whether we can really 'have it all'. My response to this is that we need to first work out for ourselves what 'all' means to us. 'All' is individual. Working out the most important things in our lives and our values, that which we care about most, takes time. When the to-do list becomes suffocating it is easy to lose sight and follow the things thrown at us and the should-dos, instead of applying conscious choice to focus on our priorities.

And so, this chapter would not be complete without, at this point, an exploration of Self-Determination Theory (SDT – be careful what order you use these letters in as I've found to my cost!). Psychologists Edward Deci and Richard Ryan have studied and written on SDT, the theory of motivation of which autonomy and competence are central elements. They describe autonomy as literally regulation by the self as opposed to heteronomy, which is control or regulation by an exterior party without the endorsement of the self. It is this self-endorsement that is critical in relation to our values. Often the debate about whether someone is truly autonomous focuses on the influence of their culture, peer group, religion and so on. In other words, the group or groups with which they identify. SDT research has been applied in the contexts of the family, schools, workplaces, religious institutions, sport teams and healthcare. In terms of geography it has been examined in Japan, South Korea, Russia, USA, Canada, Brazil and Turkey, and while across these cultures there were differences in behaviours that people see as typical of their societal norms, autonomous reasons for engaging in behaviour were uniformly associated with greater wellbeing. As Deci and Ryan conclude: *'Autonomy is a salient issue across development, life domains and cultures and is of central importance for personality functioning and wellness.'*

Can an individual exercise choice counter to the social norms of the group? Yes is the short answer (although our need to fit in and conform can make choosing to stand outside the norms of the group more difficult). We are also continually subject to priming: the non-conscious process of stimulus interpretation that leads to behavioural response. Remember the filing cabinet of our memories, the seat of our perception and onward to how we behave. Advertisers know and use priming well, as do retail psychologists who arrange a shop's products so we are guided unconsciously to spend more than we planned. The great magicians are masters at priming and distraction, controlling our attention so we miss crucial movements or gestures. But having autonomy doesn't need to be in the absence of values and interests. In fact Deci and Ryan argue: *'To be autonomous there must be some relative unity underlying one's actions; they must be congruent and endorsed by the whole self… not defined as the absence of external influences but rather by one's assent to such influences or inputs.'* [65]

Just to bring this to life, we may argue that our autonomy is compromised by the law requiring us to wear our car seat-belts, but if on reflection we endorse and place value on the need for safety and how seat-belts provide life-saving potential, wearing it does not mean we lose self-endorsed autonomy. On the other hand, a person who buys an overpriced piece of technology after watching an advert extolling its virtues but on reflection does not need it and has acted contra to their values could be said to be acting without autonomy. Personal values come from our experiences, aspirations, and other influences over the course of our lives, including teachers, parents, community, religion and our culture. They form part of our belief system and mental models of the world. They are filed and used by our brains to support the interpretation of the DRIVERS, events and others. They provide a lens, in addition to our mood-state, through which we filter the data from our senses. What we consider to be right and wrong provides part of the categorisation guidance for our filing cabinet.

Values are cohesive forces for our identity. Understanding our values allows us to bring clarity and endorsement to our choices, and as we act in line with them our sense of control and autonomy is enriched. To do this takes a bit of time but the rewards are enormous. Search on the Internet for personal values and you'll come up with an exhausting list of nouns and verbs, but there are also some useful shorter lists that can be used as a starter. Try highlighting around ten words that resonate most strongly with what is important for you. Now choose just one of them and ask yourself how you feel when this value is supported and how you feel when it is being quashed. So, for example, if a core value for you is honesty, what do you feel when you witness someone lying, or even when you lie? What priority and value do you give to your family or your health? What about learning or integrity? What happens for you when they are compromised?

When you feel energised ask yourself which value and/or priority is being supported. Likewise, when the opposite happens have a look at which of these is diminished. When they are fully established core values tend to remain pretty much fixed, but their order can change with significant emotional events that shift and re-categorise our filing cabinet of interpretation. But once you have a list of at least your top five you have further support for your personal decision tree. My family remains at the top of my values as a non-negotiable priority. Faced, for example, with a choice of advancement in my career that may adversely affect my family, my option would be clear: the family always wins. That is not to say that my work is not important; I just have a system of prioritisation drawn from my values that brings efficiency, clarity and control over the choices I make, particularly when faced by difficult ones. We all will have different decision trees that lead us on different paths. So, what has this to do with work?

Many organisations have beautifully designed posters on which their values are listed. The lists are well intended and have often been constructed with the help of evaluation by consultants. But all that well-intended work often falls a long way short of its purpose to deepen employee engagement. If you are reading this as a past or present employee, do/can you remember the values of your company? If you can pull any of the words up, what were their definitions? From the words you can recall, how did they reflect what you personally believe to be important? Did you make decisions based on these and how did you see them being enacted by those around you? If you cannot fully remember the values or cannot recall how they were portrayed within the culture, then what use were they? Then, where you may be able to remember some of them but saw behaviour counter to the espoused values, how much did this undermine your respect and trust for the organisation? Framed in six-foot-high perspex, one bank has the words integrity, trust and respect as the centrepiece of their enormous foyer – make of that what you will!

Working for an organisation whose values you do not either agree with or believe are true will undermine trust. I faced a personal experience when I landed a fantastic position as head of global communication and change at an organisation undertaking a large finance restructuring. The role played directly into my experience and strengths, but from day one I felt uncomfortable working there. It wasn't until I was speaking to a colleague about the values of the organisation alongside their product that the contradiction between the two hit me. Not only, in my opinion, were the organisation's values so far removed from their product, but also what the product did to the consumer's health sat in complete opposition to my own values. Even today I look back and find it incredulous that I didn't make this link before going for the role. Whilst I acted in line with my professional values of ensuring there was adequate handover, and I responded with honesty and integrity towards my colleagues, I left.

Events happen, internal dialogue and feelings of shame or guilt can hamper us, but choice in the way we respond, act and think is crucial to maintain our sense of self and autonomy. There are consequences to the choices we make. As one person said to me, 'I am not happy, but I can't just leave my job.' Yes, you can leave your job but as with every action there is a reaction. I'm not advocating blind risk; it is about considered paths and taking control of our next steps. Whilst socio-economic and other factors such as our capability and health play a part, people who see themselves in charge of their lives are more likely to take active steps to ensure they take opportunity for positive change and growth in the most difficult of circumstances.

Organisations that do get their values right are those that look, with those that work with and for them, at how they believe they should act in the world, from the sourcing and manufacture of their product to how they reward their staff. At Disney, the values are tangible and have led to that operational decision tree which cuts through inefficiency and provides a sense of endorsed choice and empowerment. As Roy Disney (son of Walt) simply says, 'It is not hard to make decisions once you know what your values are.'

Do your rewards motivate or demotivate?

Outside of the workplace the impact of autonomy is shown in education. The degree to which educators support autonomy is a powerful predictor of school engagement and learning outcomes.[66] Likewise in healthcare, where practitioners support autonomy there is greater involvement by the patient to their programme, and adherence and maintained change for behaviours such as stopping smoking.[67] In their study into SDT, Deci and Ryan consider autonomy as a basic psychological need and show that controlling contexts yield negative effects on wellness, whereas those that support autonomy enhance it. Organisations that seek to place rules and controls that, whilst unintentional, stifle choice, are in danger of impacting the wellbeing of their employees and will be undermining productivity. Extrinsic rewards, evaluative pressures, targets and consequential punishments can all be powerful performance constraints instead of motivators of positive behaviours. When enticing rewards are offered people can lose sight of their values and deeper needs. And when we focus on the potential of external reward we inadvertently reduce our sense of autonomy as we become subservient to, say, the bonus. When individuals are working with external rewards they tend to only do what is required rather than what they have the potential to do. Our systems of targets, service level agreements and budgeting can exercise control that caps rather than enables performance.

Another powerful force that controls our behaviour is conditional regard. We are highly motivated to be recognised by others, to be a significant part of the group in which we want to belong. But the recognition we crave from parents, teachers and managers is often kept in abeyance until certain criteria or 'conditions' are met, such as rooms being cleared, tests passed or targets met. Think about most appraisal systems geared to boxing and categorising individuals in a ranking chart, the level of which determines final remuneration. The worth of the employee becomes conditional with ever-increasing levels of targets and rules. The impacts of social environments on autonomy have been shown in several studies. For example, one study showed that people's daily wellbeing fluctuated in accordance with whether they experienced autonomy support versus control. Likewise, variations in autonomy support across intimate relationships predicted relationship satisfaction and vitality, as well as openness, agreeableness and conscientiousness.[68] These examples have been replicated in Russian and Chinese samples, confirming that this is not just a western or individualist dynamic.[69]

Which ice cream?

Choice is a good thing, but what happens when we face overwhelming choice – that sense of having no idea which way to turn? It stops us and can lead to procrastination as we circle round the options. This decision paralysis is akin to a child in an ice cream shop, offered by the parent a choice of 15 different flavours. As they try to decide between the virtues of each scoop, the reward of the ice cream and what they may miss from those that don't make it into the cone, they slow down. They get lost in amongst the choices probably around the same point that the parent starts to lose patience. If, however, only chocolate, strawberry or vanilla is presented the choice is quicker and less painful for all concerned. At work, too much choice can lead to the same paralysis and inefficiency. It's not that giving the full array of choice is wrong. In a retail experiment, it was found that too many choices discouraged consumption, but those involved reported that they enjoyed the experience more when they had more choice, despite it being more difficult to choose.[70] It's just something to be aware of when supporting decision making. Chunk up the choices, give the full details for each and anticipate the time and energy involved in the debate.

Self-efficacy

Self-efficacy is commonly referred to as one's confidence in the extent to which one can exert control over one's own behaviours, motivation and environment to achieve certain goals. Individuals with a high sense of self-efficacy set more challenging goals, persevere, visualise success and have a firmer belief in their ability to achieve. In challenging times, these individuals find ways of exerting some control, even in situations where opportunities are limited. Those that have a weaker level of self-efficacy tend to see failure ahead, looking for all the things that could go wrong so may avoid taking an opportunity to grow or find it much harder to keep going while they fight their self-doubt. This concept is aligned to Carol Dweck's work on Growth Mindset that I have explored in the chapter on Stretch. We need skills and knowledge to accomplish, but these require both self-belief and a sense of control. There is a significant difference between having the skills and applying them successfully. Albert Bandura, who is accepted as the most cited living psychologist and best known for his work on self-efficacy and social learning theory, says, 'Among the mechanisms of agency, none is more central or pervasive than people's belief about their capabilities to exercise control over their own level of functioning and over events that affect their lives. Efficacy beliefs influence how people feel, think, motivate themselves and behave.' [71]

Self-efficacy beliefs contribute to motivation in several ways: they determine the goals people set for themselves, how much effort they expend, how long they persevere in the face of difficulties, and their resilience to failures. Perceived efficacy to exercise control over stressors plays a central role in anxiety arousal. People who believe they can exercise control over threats tend not to conjure up disturbing thought patterns, whereas those who believe they cannot manage threats experience high anxiety arousal. They dwell on their deficiencies, expand the severity of potential threats, and find themselves focusing energy on things that rarely happen or are unlikely to happen.[72] In one of his research studies on the power of perceived controllability of the environment on the self-regulatory factors that govern cognitive functioning,[73] Bandura showed how quickly performance was impacted. He gave simulated tasks within an organisational context to different groups of managers. One group was instilled with the view that group behaviour was not easily influenced. They quickly lost faith in their capabilities, even when performance standards were within easy reach. They lowered their aspirations and their group's performance deteriorated. Other groups were operating with the view that group behaviour was open to influence and that they could exert a level of control over the environment. They showed high self-efficacy in the face of many challenges. They set themselves challenging goals, used good analytical thinking and achieved high levels of performance.

What if...

It is not surprising that choice and control are important for our motivation, but so much of our operating approach is to remove autonomy and exert control so that everyone complies. Guiding values are important to support organisational identity, but as businesses grow so do the rules that so often curtail the very thing they set out to achieve: motivate. How much control is exerted downward such that a perception of choice and influence is lost? What about in change, how much tends to be dictated whether directly or indirectly in terms of what will happen? How often do you hear sentences such as 'they have told us to...' or 'they have decided to...'? Whilst this reflects a devolvement of responsibility away from the person saying these words it also reveals that the individual sees a lack of choice and a diminished sense of personal influence.

What if... we look at every policy, every target and every performance management process and remove the rules? What is left?

What if... we came from the starting position that every person wants to do a good job? How can this help us as leaders to value their voice, autonomy and their approach to get it done?

What if... we changed the premise for our policies and procedures from that of 'individuals must be controlled' and replace it with 'we have the right people, let's trust them'? Is what you are measuring about your employees about control over the very few that may abuse the system or about untapping potential for the majority?

What if... we checked the values written on the posters against the real purpose of the business and the genuine values by which decisions are guided? Do they hold up? How do your customers, employees and the wider community describe how you do business? Why do people work for you? Is it for the right reasons?

CHAPTER 6

EQUITY

'*We hold these truths to be self-evident:*
that all men are created equal.'

Martin Luther King Jr

The What...

You have been working for several years with the same company. During that time your experience, knowledge and capability have been scored in the firm's performance rating system as beyond expectations. The annual appraisal is here again. It all goes well and you are satisfied with your score and review. It will mean a decent pay rise and hopefully a reasonable bonus. You chat to a colleague. She has been with the company for around a year working at the same level as you. She works hard but still has lots to learn... and yet, in your conversation you find out that her appraisal score is higher than yours and will mean she gets a greater cut of the pay pie! How do you feel?

Whilst some of you may have moved quickly to look for explanations for the difference, your first reaction is likely to have been less than positive: 'It's not fair!' Experiencing or witnessing inequity, injustice and unfairness leads to strong adverse reactions that, depending on the level of frustration, may lead to performance and relationship damaging behaviours. Let's face it, anyone who has children and observed them sharing a cake or a bounty of sweets will know the mood-piercing words, *IT'S NOT FAIR* only too well when the cut is not perceived to be absolutely the same and is often followed by a tidal wave of tears and tantrums. As with all the DRIVERS, children tell you what's up with them in no uncertain terms. But this is not the same with us grown-ups. We tend to speak through a veil of cautious politeness and professionalism. It takes skill to hear what is really being said and self-awareness to understand what you are trying to express. In the situation above, what would your reaction be? Would you – comfortable in the knowledge that there must be a clear and rational explanation for the difference – have smiled, congratulated your colleague, and, on reflection, felt not just content but happy with your own reward? Or would your first thoughts have been less congenial?

To be treated equitably is a primary need for the brain and is highly correlated to trust. A sense of fairness in and of itself can create a strong neurological reward response. Conversely, a sense of unfairness can generate a threat response that can last for days. We can feel unfairly treated by a taxi driver who takes the longer route around, or be affected by scenes and reports of inequality depicted on the news. The world is unfair, full of inequality and injustice; the distribution of wealth, resources, water and food all exemplify this. Is it fair that there is such a divide between rich and poor? Why do we treat people so terribly because of the colour of their skin or their beliefs? Whilst our levels of moral sensitivity differ and thus our responses to these questions will also differ, ultimately humans don't like unfairness and will often, if possible, seek to redress the balance, whether that involves giving to charity, seeking revenge or punishing cheats. And this is no different in the workplace.

So, two questions arise from this: 1) Why do we dislike a sense of unfairness? 2) Are we all looking for absolute equality? To understand we need to look again at whether fairness brings a survival and evolutionary benefit. Is equality necessary as a function or outcome of fairness? How does this visceral sense of what's right and wrong, just or unjust, guide our decisions and what does this mean within business? Is our view of what's fair simply a learnt sense based on our own experiences and environment? In this chapter I want to show that our own experiences do matter in our perception of what is equitable and just and that it is a deeply wired need for the brain, which is rewarded when things are fair and recoils with contempt when things are not. I want to show you that differences in treatment can exist if the process that led to the outcome is fair, and how this knowledge can be used to support intrinsic motivation and engagement in the workplace.

The biology of equity

Recent advances in cognitive science and neuroscience have allowed us insight into the impact of fairness on the brain. A lot of the research has used game theory in which participants receive and can give sums of money. One of the most famous is the Ultimatum game used in studies by Matthew Lieberman and colleagues at UCLA.[74] Participants play in pairs, and the first (the proposer) is given a sum of money, e.g. $10, and asked to split it with the second player (the target) at a level that both can agree on. If the target refuses the offer, neither player gets anything.

In the purest, most rational economic self-interest perspective, the target should accept any offer simply because he started with nothing. What are you saying to yourself at this point? 'Depends if it's fair'? Most people reject offers that are less than 20%-30% of the total – known as 'the unfair zone'. When they are offered a fair share, as perceived by the target, the reward centres of the brain light up. With the unfair offers, however, areas in the brain associated with contempt and disgust light up instead. The more this latter area lights up, the more likely the target would be to reject the offer. These results were the same when the financial reward was kept constant e.g. $2 irrespective of the total amount. But if the full amount was $4 a greater reward was detected compared to adverse reactions if the full amount were, for instance, $10. After all, a single penny fairly got is worth a thousand that are not. Importantly, these responses happen in fast-processing, automatic areas of the brain. This reaction to fairness is intuitive rather than learnt behaviour, suggesting that the brain finds self-serving behaviour emotionally unpleasant but fairness as positive and rewarding.

Another team of researchers from the Norwegian School of Economics (NHH) and brain specialists from the University of Bergen (UiB) have teamed up to explore the relationship between fairness, equality, work and money and in particular how our brains react to income distribution based on how hard people are perceived to have worked.[75] They looked at the striatum, which is considered the reward centre of the brain, setting out to prove that the brain accepts inequality if the inequality is considered fair. In other words, there can be different outcomes but if the process to reach those outcomes is considered fair then it is acceptable. They took 47 male volunteers (all male because the more similar a group of people is, the easier it is to record any differences) and asked them to perform simple office work for 30, 60 or 90 minutes. The participants were then paired up. They were paired according to the amount of time they had worked. A volunteer who had worked for 30 minutes was teamed with a 90-minute worker and a 60-minute worker was paired with another 60-minute worker. They were then presented with 51 different distributions of Norwegian Kroner (NOK) split between themselves and their partner and were asked to evaluate each distribution to indicate how much they liked or disliked it. While they did this, their brain's activity was measured using a fMRI scanner. The results showed that the striatum's response to how much money they received was dependent on how much they had worked. This study was the first to look at the neuronal response to inequality and whether being treated differently was fair or unfair. Fair inequality, it turns out, is OK for our brain.

Our decisions are so subject to fairness that we would rather go without than accept an unfair distribution, with a tendency towards acting in ways to try to remove or limit those who take more than their fair share. Think about the public outcry surrounding Lance Armstrong's drug cheating – a condemnation that came even from people who were not cycling enthusiasts. We want to uncover and punish cheats and liars and we can seek revenge to being wronged or disadvantaged. I played a card game called Cheat, aptly named as it turned out, with my children recently. The idea of the game is to get rid of your cards before anyone else. To do so each player places a card face down and calls out its number. The next player then must place a card that is either equal to, one below, or one above the number. Because the cards are placed faced down, trust is needed to accept what the player says, but players aren't obliged to be truthful. If another player suspects foul play they call 'cheat!' If they are proved right the perpetrator has to pick up all the cards on the table; if they are wrong and there has been no cheat, then the player who made the accusation has to pick up.

As I played I noticed my feelings and I observed my children. We all knew it was a game and yet when a cheat was uncovered I felt a jolt of annoyance – particularly if the cheat affected my go. I saw and heard the outward manifestation of this jolt on the faces and in the words of my daughters when they were affected. The game punishes the person that falsely accuses and therefore undermines trust, but also the one that cheats. And the punishment is both actual in terms of picking up the cards and neurological. Of course, it is the emotions that make for a good game, but even in a game in which we are rationally fully aware of what we are doing and why, we cannot switch off the primary mid-brain threat response to unfairness.

We are not the only creatures with a sense of fairness. Dr Frans De Waal, Dutch primatologist and ethnologist, has carried out research to demonstrate that fair play is sought amongst other species. An experiment on Capuchin monkeys showed that subjects preferred receiving nothing to receiving a reward that was unfair in relation to that given to a peer monkey. The study uses two monkeys from the same group who expect to be treated equally. Following a simple task, the first monkey is given a rock and gives it back to the researcher. For this the monkey receives a piece of cucumber, which he eats contently because monkeys like cucumber. Then the researcher asks the second monkey to do the same with a same size rock but this time he gets a much more coveted grape as his reward. The first monkey sees this.

The researcher gets the first monkey to carry out the rock exercise again, and again he gets a piece of cucumber. This time though the first monkey rejects the cucumber, throwing it back at the researcher. The test is carried out again with the second monkey receiving a grape and the first cucumber. Now the first monkey has had enough. He directs his anger and frustration at the researcher, aiming the cucumber right back at her then shaking his cage in rage. Anthropologists suggest that this research indicates a biological and evolutionary sense of social fair play, and similar experiments have been carried out on dogs, birds, elephants and chimps. Look up De Waal's study on YouTube, it's very funny and is a great example of the inbuilt aversion we have to unfairness. As you watch, relate the reaction and behaviour back to aspects at work such as bonus allocation, appraisal ranking or other reward mechanisms.

So why do we need and want fairness?

Our pursuit of fairness and negative reaction to inequity has been researched for many years and is often termed inequity aversion. In 1999, Fehr and Schmidt wrote their paper 'A theory of fairness, competition and cooperation'. They showed that disadvantageous inequity aversion shows up in us as the *willingness to sacrifice potential gain to block another individual from receiving a superior reward*.[76] If we think about this with children again, imagine giving your daughter £5 and her brother £15 and telling them they were not allowed to share the total between them – what is going to be the result? If you then say she may choose for her brother to not have the money but that means she may not have hers either, what do you think she will say? As before, economically and rationally she should accept to keep the money as is, but if she does it is likely to be with resentment and negative memories that will last for a long time. It is more likely that she will choose for both her and her brother to have nothing and feel better because she has served justice and redressed the balance.

This evolutionary hard-wiring for fairness makes sense to me. How can you build a society where behaviour is inherently self-serving? We survive and have thrived in terms of evolutionary supremacy because of our ability to cooperate. If we only looked after number one, then where would we be? Resource allocation would be skewed and free-riders would take advantage where they could. This of course does happen and there is, as I've said, a great deal of inequity in the world with a very small minority having claim over most of the world's spoils. But ultimately, from a survival perspective, if we think of the small communities in which we lived, to be able to share, play fair, support an equitable process that builds cooperation and rejects injustice meant that we were more able to create an environment for stability and growth where everyone thrives. Another theory about why fairness is so important to us looks at evolutionary history where we needed to trade resources through favours. The value of resources yet to be received or to be provided was stored in individual memory. Fairness and equitable exchange thus equated to survival. We had to build strong detectors for cheats. Breaking the social rules of equity for personal gain destroys the fabric of cooperation, fundamental for human co-existence, which secures individual survival. Serving others is self-serving.

There have been a few games devised over the years. The Dictator game, which as it suggests places one player in the seat of power to decide the split with no consequences. The Ultimatum game, as I've described above, which gives the person receiving the offer from the first player the choice to veto the entire deal should he see it as unfair, leaving both parties with nothing and effectively punishing the first player through self-sacrifice. And the Trust game when the initial endowment to the dictator is given by his or her partner and which requires the partner to trust that the dictator will return something. These have all been used to evidence inequity aversion. In 2005, John List looked to counter the evidence for inequity by modifying these experiments, giving one player the option to steal money from the other player. He gave both players money with the choice to give to, or take any amount of money from the other; only 10% gave anything and 40% opted to take all the other's money. For me, in these last experiments, List set up a situation where trust is removed before the individuals have a chance to assess things for themselves. In the absence of trust the natural behaviour is defensive – keep all, grab all, defend all and give away nothing.

Despite the global injustice and the many forms it takes, we desire to live in a more equal society. The Harvard professor Michael Norton has studied public opinion on this matter.[77] He first looked at the CEO pay gap to manual workers and then asked thousands of individuals to comment on what they thought it was and what they would like it to be. He then measured the results against what the gap actually is. A total of 55,000 people around the globe took part across many countries. What they thought the pay gap was significantly underestimated the reality. And against what they thought was the correct level the majority felt a lower ratio would in fact be fairer.

Norton had previously looked at wealth distribution with the behavioural economist Dan Ariely in 2011. They asked Americans what they believed wealth distribution was across the country and what they would like it to be, and measured this again against reality. The participants estimated the top 20% of households owned about 59% of the country's net worth. The actual is they own 84%. When asked to describe what they would like it to be the results were as with the CEO pay gap: far more equal a spread than what they had estimated it to be. In the same experiment, people were shown two pie charts of wealth split: one from Sweden which is far more egalitarian and then one based on the US wealth split which is far more skewed to the rich. 92% of the Americans asked said they would want to live in the Swedish model.[78] Gallup too has found in their research that Americans believe wealth should be distributed more evenly, with 52% in support of implementing heavy taxation on the rich to achieve this end. This result is virtually the same as when Gallup first explored this question in 1984.[79]

Michael Norton said, 'People drastically underestimate the current disparities in wealth and income in their societies... and their ideals are more equal than their estimates. Maybe more importantly people from all walks of life... rich or poor, all over the world, have a large degree of consensus in their ideals. Everyone's ideals are more equal than the way they think things are.'

Elizabeth Tricomi, professor of psychology at Rutgers University in New Jersey, with a team of researchers at Caltech and Trinity College Institute of Neuroscience in Dublin, looked at our reactions to how fairness played out when the playing field started at different levels. They took 40 male subjects, paired them up, and gave each one $30. Each was then asked to draw from a hat a ball that had either 'rich' or 'poor' on it. Those that picked 'rich' then received $50 extra. (What is your reaction to this?) The researchers then monitored the participants' brains as they transferred money to each other. What they found was increased activity in the reward centres of the brain (striatum and pre-frontal cortex) when the 'rich' players transferred money to others compared to when they received money. However, the 'poor' subjects' brains gave opposite results. The brain scans show that on a neurological level we take social information and react to advantageous and disadvantageous inequality, which, as with Norton's work, suggests that we prefer a financial equality or, at the very least, narrower gaps – a neurological rebalancing of the books. Tricomi said of the study, 'Overall, it looks like these regions were responding most when the outcome would be the most fair, and the least when the outcome would be the least fair... our study shows that the brain doesn't just reflect self-interested goals, but instead, these basic reward processing regions of the brain seem to be affected by social information. That might explain why what happens to other people seems to matter so much to us, even when it might not actually directly affect us.'

Do you give to charities that perhaps are not directly linked to your own situation? How do you feel when you give a donation? How do you feel when the playing field is unfair? What do you notice when you cheat – what emotions raise their heads... guilt, shame? What is your reaction when you witness someone else cheating for personal benefit?

A fair society

So, within us all there appears to be a desire for fairness, something that is part of how we are wired, and yet we can override the neurological signals and still behave for self-interest.

Many political ideologies have as part of their foundations a strategy for fairness across society. The French economist Tomas Piketty, the author of the bestselling book *Capital in the Twenty-First Century*, focuses his research on wealth and income inequality in Europe and the United States. He argues that when the rate of return on capital is greater than the rate of economic growth, over the long term it results in a concentration of wealth, and this unequal distribution causes social and economic instability. His solution is a global system of progressive wealth taxes to bring about greater wealth equilibrium. Socialism has its roots in a social and economic system characterised by social ownership whereby production and the economy is cooperatively managed to meet the demands and needs of the people.

In 1963, John Stacey Adams put forward the Equity Theory,[80] a principle of balance and fairness where an employee's motivation is correlated to their perception of equity, fairness and justice as practised by their leaders and managers in the workplace. The test for this is simple: is what I contribute to the organisation (time, skills, enthusiasm, ideas etc.) fair in relation to what I receive from the organisation (recognition, pay, benefits, development etc.), and is what others are contributing and receiving fair in relation to my input and return? The simplicity of this model has been criticised, with dissenters arguing that there are bound to be many variables affecting one individual's perception of fairness at any one time. When writing about the Equity Theory, the business guru Peter Drucker explained how '*The basic idea behind the Equity Theory is that workers, in an attempt to balance – what they put into their jobs and what they get out – will unconsciously assign values to each of their various contributions, for example: experience, relationships, personal strengths… Hence, according to the Equity Theory, the most highly motivated employees are those who perceive rewards as being equal to their contributions, and also the feeling that they are being rewarded at a comparable rate as co-workers… This does not mean that every manager should treat every employee identically, since workers tend to measure contributions in different ways.*'

Karl Marx was a philosopher studying politics and economics. He analysed the class system and the complex relationships between the 'haves' and 'have-nots' – or the capitalists and the proletariat or workers. His argument was that this class struggle and divide would ultimately lead to a more socialist and classless society – the more extreme version of this being communism where class does not exist – wherein the socio-economic structure is all based on common ownership without money or the state.

All of these standpoints seem to me to build their teachings on a desire for a level playing field. Capitalism differs insofar as it is fundamentally about production and the mechanisms of production being often privately, not socially, owned. Trade is for profit, competition is the bedrock of trade, and capital is for accumulating. The West has mainly supported a capitalist and individualistic structure, promoting the pursuit of one's own goals, valuing independence and self-reliance over the social group, whereas many eastern countries predominantly seek a collective strategy which emphasises the importance of the community. Even as far back as the 18ᵗʰ century, Adam Smith, philosopher and recognised founder of economics who through his 'invisible hand' metaphor detailed the balance of supply and demand with enough profit as an incentive to adjust production, based his philosophy in moral terms where justice and freedom, particularly for the poor, prospered. Smith was a staunch critic of capitalism whose concern for fairness over economic efficiency branded any strategy that protects producer profits – such as direct subsidies or competition restricting regulations – as a 'veil of taxes upon the poor'. He said that 'crony capitalism' was akin to a referee changing the results of the game to suit his favoured players. *'To hurt in any degree the interest of any one order of citizens for no other purpose but to promote that of some other is evidently contrary to that justice and equality of treatment which the sovereign owes to all the different orders of his subjects.'* [81]

Social democracy is yet another political view that seeks to bring together economic and social interventions that support social justice and the regulation of the economy and redistribution of income in the general interest within a capitalist framework. Western individualistic self-serving capitalism has certainly dominated several major economies and we have all seen and been affected by the damage caused in its wake. Whatever your political views, it will be interesting to see if collective, social democracy becomes a greater force as we seek a better, sustainable approach that sits comfortably with our own neurological make-up for a more equal and fair society.

The effect of unfairness on our decisions

A sense of fairness affects our decisions. There is a great deal of research that looks at the neurological basis for ethical decision making. One of the first studies where people made real decisions with real consequences was carried out by researchers at Caltech.[82] Twenty-six men and women aged between 28 and 55 were given a real-life dilemma. Each was given short biographies of 60 orphans at the Canaan Children's Home in Uganda. The orphanage would receive a donation depending on the decisions made by the subjects. Whilst being scanned using fMRI machines they were each given about eight seconds to decide how to distribute meals among groups of children within different scenarios. For example, in one scenario they could either give four extra meals to each of two children or six extra meals to one child; those that weren't chosen received nothing. Or, the children had been allocated extra meals and the participants had to decide if it was better to take six meals away from each of two children or ten meals away from one. The results showed the reward centres lighting when the participants gave out meals. The insula region, the hub for moderating social cognition, empathy and reward-driven decision making, activated more when they took them away. Stephen Quartz, associate professor at Caltech, suggested that the inequity of the choices triggered the insula. He said, 'The emotional response to unfairness pushes people from extreme inequity and drives them to be fair.'

Interestingly, this study showed a large variation in brain activity across the participants, indicating the individual differences in perception of inequity driving the response. Whilst unfairness is hard-wired there is a filter on our interpretation of events based on our values and worldview, which will form our ultimate perception of the situation and inevitably lead to differing opinions. In other words, in any given event what's fair to me may not be fair to you. Depending on your preferences, beliefs and values, which are established from your own experiences, culture, education, parenting and so on, you may evaluate fairness and justice in different situations with the following criteria:

- Everyone should be treated exactly the same

- Those that have worked harder and/or taken greater risk should receive a greater contribution relative to the effort/ risk

- Those at disadvantage (poverty, discrimination, capability, disability etc.) should be allowed extra support or compensation to level the field

- Those that don't play by the rules, lie or cheat should be punished

Understanding that a perception of fairness is part of our biological make-up and how our own values inform that perception gives us self-insight and provides us with a starting point to try to understand others' reactions when they perceive unfairness.

So What?

Unfairness and injustice appear to also affect our health. One Dutch study looked at whether low justice at work increased the risk of depression. Over 4,000 non-depressed employees across 378 different work units within the public services took part in 2007. They completed surveys that assessed their perception of procedural and relational justice in their workplace, took part in personal interviews, and had their concentration levels of the stress hormone cortisol analysed. In 2009, over 3,000 were followed up. The results showed that working in a work unit with low justice predicted the onset of depression. Importantly this study showed that workload did not correlate to an increased risk of depression but that the environment in which the employee worked did.[83]

A similar study was carried out between Stockholm University and the University of East Anglia. This time it spanned 5,800 employees working in Sweden. It found that when an employee's assessment of procedural justice at work changed, including processes that determined their rewards, pay, promotion etc., so did their assessment of their health. Those reporting more positive perceptions of justice also reported their health more positively. Conversely, those with poorer perceptions of justice reported more negative evaluations of their health. Dr Constanze Eib who led the study said of the results, 'If people feel unfairly treated, they not only decrease their performance, they might become a less good employee by coming in late or taking extended lunch breaks. It is serious from the individual perspective in terms of their health, and for the organisation because it affects business performance and how long people stay in a workplace.'

In the workplace, responses to perceived injustice often take the form of silent acts that directly affect the other person involved, such as refusing to help the offending colleague or manager or perhaps doing the work more slowly. Gossip can ensue as the employee seeking justice looks to add collaborators to their cause. We can seek retaliation through acts of revenge to punish the perpetrator, particularly when we believe that they have gained over others through their acts. A Harvard University study explored this desire to punish. They grouped 560 volunteers into pairs of cheaters and non-cheaters, and had the partners play a simple game over the Internet. For all the teams, cheaters could choose to 'steal' 20 cents from their non-cheating partners, and then the non-cheaters had the option of paying 10 cents to 'punish' the thief by reducing their partner's wealth by 30 cents. In one third of the teams, the cheater stealing 20 cents would still mean they had less money than their partner. In another third of the teams, stealing would result in the partners having equal wealth. Only in the last group did stealing 20 cents make the cheater's wealth surpass that of the non-cheater.

In the first two scenarios, roughly the same proportion of non-cheaters paid to punish cheaters, and they did this regardless of whether or not the cheaters had actually chosen to cheat. (According to the researchers, this was the 'baseline' of punishments — punishing wasn't correlated with actually cheating.) But among the third group, when the cheating partners' wealth would surpass the non-cheaters', punishment more than doubled. These results make a strong case for the idea that the decision to punish stems from our aversion to unfairness. We dislike it when cheating enables one person to get ahead of someone else that didn't cheat. But if the cheater's ploy didn't get them very far, we don't become nearly so angry. We ultimately punish out of a desire for fairness and rebalance not purest revenge.[84]

Whatever the course of action, the result of inequity and unfairness is detrimental to intrinsic motivation and engagement. If a perception of unfairness continues, research has shown that there is a significant relationship to psychosomatic health complaints and absenteeism.[85] Viewed from any angle, unfairness and injustice are performance blockers, injecting risk into decision making and relationships.

Inequity and unfairness matters.

What if...

So, the perception of unfairness has a direct impact on motivation and performance. Much has been done to mitigate the effect of unconscious bias in decision making, whether that be in recruitment, promotion or performance assessment, and this helps to reduce inequity but we need to go further.

What if... we started to really listen, learning to recognise when individuals are demonstrating their sense of unfairness? When you know that the perception of the individual in reaction to an event is that of unfairness, even if you are unable to relate to it, it will identify a reason for demotivation and lead to a conversation to uncover the root causes from which, hopefully, action can then be taken to address the issues.

What if... we recognised and rewarded on team outcome and reduced the spotlight on the individual? All for one and one for all.

What if... we really closed the pay gap between the top and the bottom of the hierarchy? Every role has a part to play and we know that there is a desire to live within a more egalitarian society. While the rich get richer and the poor poorer we'll never achieve the world that we say we want.

CHAPTER 7
RELIABILITY

'*When you accept what is, every moment is the best moment.*'

Eckhart Tolle

The What...

Are you facing a change somewhere in your life? How are you feeling – excited, nervous? What are you thinking about the change: Can I do this? What does it mean for me? A great opportunity? How are you behaving?

Have you ever been in a social situation in which you are not sure how to behave or what the etiquette is? How did you feel – uncomfortable, a little lost?

How reliable is your world? Is everything predictable, certain, secure? How much time do you spend planning the future, writing lists, organising things that perhaps you don't have direct influence over – whether that's tomorrow, next year or maybe even for retirement? How much energy do you invest in trying to instil certainty in your life?

We are the stories we tell ourselves

Our brain pattern matches the stimulus it receives with the experiences it stores. I mentioned the filing cabinet in our mid-brain at the beginning of the book so I will take you back to this now. This filing cabinet stores all of you: your memories, your experiences, everything that has happened to you. The filing system is ordered by association and subdivided by level of 'safety' or 'threat'. The emotion experienced with an event is the determinant for the order, the chemical librarian. So, for someone who was stung badly by a bee as a child, bees will be stored in the threat category. In the same category, because of association, certain places will be filed next to bees – maybe parks because that's where you were when you got stung. The threats are placed in order of danger based on the peaks of emotional response experienced at the time of the encounter. This filing process establishes a pattern for interpretation. Long after the details of the event have disappeared, the brain has a frame for avoidance even if, in this example, there are no bees to be seen and rationally you know parks are not dangerous.

Events don't need to have happened directly to you to have placed a threat file in your cabinet; for some people tall buildings and planes flying overhead are interpreted as threatening even though they were not anywhere near the Twin Towers on 9/11. Hoodies with rucksacks, tattoos, skinheads, and flowers – various things can form links from the original information being received, filed by safety or threat, to an action of avoidance in the future. And it's not about the rational in terms of making sense of the order of the files, it is emotional reasoning: a highly attuned mechanism for survival which is the basis of our beliefs, biases and our rules about the world.

We can change or we can strengthen our beliefs and the stories we tell ourselves about events. Imagine that I ask you to present to an auditorium of people about a subject that you know about. As I speak the words you may reach into your filing cabinet and pull out the file that tells you how well you have done in previous talks you've given, that you know and feel comfortable about the subject, and you have been looking for an opportunity to demonstrate your knowledge. This pattern of interpretive thoughts will trigger positive emotions – maybe excitement and confidence. These emotions will drive your behaviour and physical reaction, such as holding your voice firm and heart rate steady. You have comfort in what I ask you to do and certainty about how things will play out. This isn't the reaction, however, for many. As I ask you this, most people reach subconsciously into their cabinet and pull out presentations often filed slap-bang next to dentists. The pattern matched is that of threat. Your heart rate increases, palms become sweaty, thoughts about the subject become cloudy and your voice becomes shaky. You get butterflies and feel sick. The presentation is unlikely to go well. If you avoid giving the presentation you will reinforce the position of the original filing. If you give the presentation and it doesn't go so well, then guess what, you'll strengthen that pattern and may even re-file presentations to a higher category of risk.

This file and retrieval process ensures that we don't need to analyse every situation in the moment. It is non-conscious, incredibly fast and efficient, and allows us to go about our day; but while there is a clear survival advantage to this fast track process, just as with the presentation, it can get in the way. There is an opportunity cost associated with speed, namely accuracy. Experiences with a difficult customer, boss, presentations or targets can all have a threat file. The interpretation of danger perhaps triggered when we have only seen a name appear in the inbox can lead to unhelpful thoughts, physical symptoms and behaviour. We are the stories we tell ourselves scripted from the files of our experience, but we also have the power to change the stories and reorder the files establishing more helpful patterns of thinking, feeling and behaving. To do this we must first understand our patterns, to become aware of them, before we can change them – tough when they are not conscious but cognitive techniques can support the process of developing emotional literacy.

Memory

In his book *Intelligence,* Jeff Hawkins details how the brain functions like a prediction machine. Hawkins, who pioneered the development of PDAs such as the Palm and Treo, seeks to build software to mimic the brain's functionality and suggests that prediction is central to the brain's development. The concept of his memory prediction framework is that bottom-up inputs are matched in a hierarchy of recognition and evoke a series of top-down expectations encoded as potentiations. It involves the hippocampus and thalamus as the memory pattern stores (the drawers of your filing cabinet) and leads to predictions to what will happen next. When an input sequence matches a memorised sequence at a given layer (each hierarchy level remembers frequently observed temporal sequences of input patterns and generates labels or 'names' for these sequences), a 'name' is propagated from which expectation is created. When, however, a mismatch between input and memorised sequences occurs, a more complete representation propagates upwards to provide alternative interpretation.[86] Put all this another way using the filing cabinet analogy, information received is matched to a file, which in turn feeds back what's going to happen next. When there is not a perfect match to a file, the closest possible is chosen and other drawers are opened to try to come up with what it could be and what might happen. Memories have to be learnt, they are not pre-wired, and so this process of extraction, retrieval and reconstruction happens continually.

You assess millions of pieces of information every moment but only a few make it to your conscious awareness. Things, objects, others' actions that are assessed as safe and benign are effectively consciously ignored. It's what Daniel Kahneman refers to as your 'experiencing self' – fast, intuitive, unconscious mode of thinking that operates in the present moment, focusing on the quality of our experience. He shows us how each moment of the 'experiencing self' lasts about three seconds, most of them vanishing without a trace. Ever been in a room where until someone points out the picture on the wall you'd not noticed it? Or couldn't remember if you'd locked the car only to go back and see that you had, as you always automatically do? Your brain has clocked all of this but it doesn't need to invoke a behavioural response to information, which is both safe and non-relevant. The other side to this is what Kahneman refers to as our 'remembering self': these are the memories you store, the files you set up, the categorisations and associations you compile for retrieval later. These memories are the intense moments we experience within an event, the emotional peaks, particularly how it ends. To 'leave on a high' as the saying goes has scientific credence. To leave a holiday when you still want to stay will form a more positive memory of the whole.

Our memories are retrieved and put back together for survival, not for deploying irrefutable facts in a court of law, something that the legal system must deal with in relation to eyewitness testimony. We are subject to priming, where exposure to one stimulus influences the response to another, tapping into our memory associations that correspond to what we expect to see next – the filing cabinet again. If I ask you to complete the missing letters in the word R**n but had preceded this with the word damp or wet you are more likely to think of Rain than Ruin. Psychologist Elizabeth Loftus of the University of California refutes that memory is like videotape but that it is constructed and reconstructed to create a story that appears correct to our conscious self. She has shown how memory reconstruction can be distorted based on information that precedes its retrieval such as which questions are asked of witnesses about events. Loftus says of memory that it is like a Wikipedia page – you can go there and change it, but so can other people. In her experiments eyewitnesses were asked to estimate how fast a car was going before a crash. If the word 'smashed' was used in the preceding question the participants said the cars were going significantly faster and were more likely to describe broken glass when there was in fact none. One project in the United States gathered information on 300 people convicted of crimes they didn't commit. After many years in prison, DNA testing has in most cases proved their innocence. When these cases were analysed, three quarters were due to faulty eyewitness memory.

What is reality?

The brain undertakes huge effort to construct our reality, the interpretation of which can shift moment to moment. How tired we feel, our resilience situation to situation, our health, priming cues and mood all shade the filter through which it extracts the answers from the filing cabinet often leading to differing views of the same event. Whilst different parts of the brain specialise in sound, colour and so on, our interpretation draws on the full matrix of networks to establish a complete picture of what is happening and to predict what is about to happen. Your reality is based on what is already in your files and is only updated by the information received via your senses instead of rebuilding reality moment to moment. Your brain makes assumptions about what is out there and unless told differently will fill in the gaps for you. It means the filing cabinet process remains efficient in the face of billions of pieces of data that need to be continually filtered. Most often your brain delivers up to you what it expects to see and not necessarily actual reality. It's why yuor brain can raed tihs and this...

It deson't mttaer in waht oredr the ltteers in a wrod aepapr, the olny iprmoatnt tihng is taht the frist and lsat ltteer are in the rghit pcale. The rset can be a toatl mses and you can sitll raed it wouthit pobelrm.

S1M1L4RLY, Y0UR M1ND 15 R34D1NG 7H154U70M471C4LLY W17H0U7 3V3N 7H1NK1NG 4B0U7 17.

Our filing cabinet may not always be perfect and will get its interpretation wrong but, on the whole, the system is fast, efficient and has been effective for our survival for over a millennium or two. Our capacity to reappraise the story that our mid-brain provides, as I described at the beginning of this book, gives us the power to choose a different response. Resilience and optimal decision making comes from our ability to use our emotional unconscious alongside our conscious rational mind. As Albert Einstein said, 'The intuitive mind is a sacred gift and the rational mind is a faithful servant. We have created a society that honours the servant and has forgotten the gift.'

So What?

Reliability is part of our survival mechanism

We crave reliability, a sense of certainty and put energy into finding control to mitigate ambiguity. Whilst the tolerance of uncertainty and ambiguity will differ with individuals, the brain feels safe when it gets what's going on and can predict what happens next. The concept of 'tolerance of ambiguity' was first developed by Frenkel-Brunswick in 1948 and has since been a subject for much research. Psychologists split ambiguity and uncertainty although both research and common sense show that they interrelate. For clarity, I will refer to ambiguity as the reaction to a situation in the present whilst uncertainty refers to behaviours in response to the uncertainty of the future. I use reliability to encompass both a perception of uncertainty and ambiguity. If we cannot pattern match what is happening or what is to about to happen the threat circuitry is triggered.

Unreliability is like a torn map: without the missing piece the whole landscape cannot be understood and the next steps cannot be calculated. fMRI scanning has shown that the level of ambiguity in choices correlates positively with activation in the amygdala and orbitofrontal cortex – areas associated with threat – and negatively with activation in the striatal system – the reward centre.[87] In the absence of information, we seek to fill in the gaps to make sense of the ambiguity and uncertainty. Even if we fill it with information that turns out to be wrong, at the time it provides the brain with comfort. This is termed unimaginatively as 'information seeking behaviour'.

This need for information to establish reliability has been found in studies with primates. Ethan Bromberg-Martin and Okihide Hikosaka showed through their research[88] on monkeys that there is a distinct preference for information now. The experiment gave monkeys options to choose between coloured targets, one with information about future reward and the other blank. The monkeys were then given the targets one at a time. Their brain scans revealed that the dopamine neurons responded more strongly to the targets carrying the advance information about what was to happen next. We simply want to know – and now. We strive to reveal the details of the surprise, what's in the wrapped gift, and what the leadership are planning at work. Ignorance is not bliss when our brains are attempting to work out how to keep us alive.

Our power of prediction

The predictive power of the brain can be seen in the world of sport. In tennis, cricket and even boxing the movements of flying objects, from balls to punches, travel faster than our conscious processing speed. A cricket ball travels at 90 miles per hour. It will take 500 milliseconds to travel the 22-yard wicket. A tennis ball travelling at 140 miles per hour will reach its opponent on the baseline in less than 400 milliseconds. In these split seconds, the batsman and tennis player need to assess the direction and speed of the ball and initiate motor reaction to succeed and yet the pace of the action is quicker than we can consciously calculate. Muhammad Ali, when fighting George Foreman, threw his punches from beginning to end in 166 milliseconds. If we took the time to think about what to do we'd be out cold – literally! Is that why the mid-off position in cricket is preceded with 'silly'?

Now imagine being faced with a lion, 100 feet away. Travelling at 50 miles per hour it will sink its teeth into you in just over a second. The line between death and survival came down to a few thousandths of a second. To deal with this we developed subconscious pre-attentive information processing for automatic motor responses. What we consciously 'see' is past news footage because our subconscious brains have already made the assessment and activated the appropriate physical movements through prediction and anticipation. Rafael

Nadal will have made many subconscious anticipatory judgments based on the way his opponent's feet are positioned and the speed of the court even before the ball has left Andy Murray's tennis racket.

George Kolreiser, psychologist and ex-hostage negotiator, tells a story from the research of Gary Klein of the power of this predictive process in his book *Hostage at the Table*.[89] A fire chief led his team under all the normal safety protocols into a house to put out a kitchen fire. As he stood in the hallway he ordered his men straight back out again. The men escaped just before the whole of the ground floor collapsed into the inferno that raged beneath them. When asked about his decision the chief couldn't explain why he just knew they were not safe – he reacted with no apparent conscious thought or rationale. When he explored this experience a little later he was able to piece together some of the information that had flowed from what he faced in the house, all of which had been matched subconsciously to his memory files built over many years of experience. The heat was 'all wrong' and the noise muffled. Whilst smoke was clearly coming from the kitchen seemingly indicating the source of the fire, the information was not lining up. Investigations later showed that the fire had started in the basement and had started to come through the kitchen floor. Had the fire chief not got his men out there would have been a very different ending to the story. His brain was able to assess and pattern match the data points to then predict what was likely to happen next, leading to an instruction to his physical self to escape – and all before he was consciously aware.

Our tolerance of unreliability

In a direct survival event, such as that the fire chief faced, the ability to recognise, predict and react is clearly invaluable. But situations happen every day that, although not life-threatening, increase the unreliability in our lives, leading to differing levels of discomfort and avoidance. Adrian Furnham and Joseph Marks, in their review of the literature on this subject,[90] noted that those who are intolerant of ambiguity tend to be black and white in their thinking because the variability of the truth of the matter is too difficult to assess. They stick rigidly to what they understand even if it is unhelpful or incorrect.[91] Better the devil you know! At the other end of the spectrum, those who score high on the 'Openness to Experience scale'[92] perceive ambiguity as desirable and can show sensation-seeking and risk-taking behaviour.[93] Other scales such as Hofstede's 'Uncertainty Avoidance Index'[94] and Freeston's 'Intolerance of Uncertainty Scale'[95] all look at an individual's trait around their reaction to reliability.

We all approach uncertainty or ambiguity with varied levels of caution, feeling threat or discomfort, excitement, or a buzz from the challenge. In Furnham's literature review he lists findings from many studies that look at differing levels of tolerance of ambiguity. Examples of what he lists are that high tolerance of ambiguity (TA) is positively correlated to better performance and CEOs with high TA were related to firms with higher financial and market performance. Intolerance of ambiguity is negatively correlated with life satisfaction and positively correlated with anxiety. Our genes play a part predisposing us to traits of preferred reactions and thoughts about what's happening around and to us. Our genetics, however, as with all things, is not the full story. Often our pattern of thinking and the way we organise our files comes from learning and is written into our neural circuitry by our experiences. In addition to those experiences, how we perceive a situation will be dependent on everything from our mood, how tired we are, our competence, the situation, the meaning we place on the elements within the event, our values or other worries and distractions at the time. How we then react to perceived unreliability will depend on our coping strategies, our level of optimism, our social support, and our ability to see stress as a challenge. Whilst our trait will give us the starting point, the rest of the pathway to how the brain interprets levels of threat when faced with ambiguity and uncertainty will be set by other factors which we can control and modify.

All move

So, let's take a situation. Imagine you are asked to move your desk position from the place by the lift that you have occupied for the last two years to one just by the window about ten feet away. You may be in a pretty good mood. Other desk moves have gone reasonably smoothly and where you sit at work is not hugely important to you – after all, if you can get the work done what does it matter? Your reaction to this request may provide an immediate sense of uncertainty but it quickly evaporates and you get on with sorting out the move. If, however, as for many, this seemingly small change delivers heightened discomfort, it may lead to a very different reaction as your brain is unable to pattern match the new unknown position (let alone the other DRIVERS this situation quashes). In my experience, desk moves can be incredibly emotive, arousing behaviours like gossip and questioning: Why am I moving? Who will I sit next to? The emotional reaction outweighing the rational – after all, it is only a desk, isn't it? The issue is all about uncertainty throwing the mid-brain into a tailspin. And, while questions circle seeking to regain certainty, performance declines and can stop completely as attention focuses on the move.

It's why hot-desking is such an uncomfortable prospect, loathed by many. Whilst it is an obvious and rational space and money saver within the accounting system, it can also send the mid-brain into a frenzy. The uncertainty triggered by hot-desking leads to behaviours from taking time to set up the new desk before work starts with photos, pencils, laptops, putting everything in the same position each time to seeking out and commandeering certain desks with tactics such as hanging coats on the backs of chairs – the office equivalent of the towel on the sun-bed. All of this takes time and, although I know of no study considering the efficiency of productivity while hot-desking, I would bet that at least 15 minutes per person is spent on these types of ambiguity-mitigating activities every time they use a new desk. Add that up in hours spent per employee per year and then compare that to the figures saved in the accounts. That's not to say that I'm anti hot-desking as a concept. I've spent too many years leading finance operations and logistics to not understand the benefits; it's simply that it doesn't – just like so many well-intentioned plans in business – take into consideration how humans respond to unreliability.

The science behind the lucky charm

Do you have a lucky charm? A routine that you perform to secure success? Sometimes, because of associative learning, we ritualistically perform and re-perform certain behaviours because we irrationally believe them to provide a semblance of control over the future. Sports players, musicians and actors are renowned for their 'lucky' routines and objects. Michael Jordan wore his university shorts under his team shorts because he had worn them when he led UNC to the NCAA Championships in 1982. Bjorn Borg won Wimbledon five times in a row between 1976 and 1980. To prepare for this event he grew a 'lucky' beard and always wore the same striped Fila shirt. And, sticking with tennis, Serena Williams, seen as one of the most aggressive and successful female players of all time, puts much of her achievement down to her routines, which include tying her shoelaces in a specific way and bouncing the ball five times before her first serve and twice before her second. Of course, be careful to never mention the name of the Scottish play to an actor or wish them good luck – better to tell them to 'break a leg'. As a dancer for many years, that last one always seemed particularly strange to me!

These 'luck'-inducing and seemingly irrational behaviours spuriously predict future outcomes for these artists and athletes as each ritual performed is linked by the mid-brain to greater certainty with the aid of superstitious forces. Yet there is some science to the routines and charms because they serve to dampen some of the nerves that could hinder performance, helping to boost confidence. Many of us pay credence to lucky charms and superstitions. Don't walk under ladders, hunt for four-leaf clovers or say good morning to single magpies – all of which have no influence on actual events but do go some way to relieving us of niggling worries or uncertainties. It does something else too. When we convince ourselves of 'lucky' associations we relax our minds and so open them up to opportunity.

Professor of psychology Richard Wiseman has spent years researching luck, culminating in his book *The Luck Factor*.[96] His studies on lucky and unlucky individuals reveal that those perceived as 'lucky' are no luckier than anyone else; they simply see, understand and act on opportunities presented to them. In one experiment he asked people to read a newspaper and work out how many photographs were inside. He had secretly put a message halfway in that read '*Stop counting – there are 43 photographs in this newspaper.*' [97] Wiseman said, 'It was staring everyone in the face but the unlucky individuals tended to miss it and the lucky people spotted it... [the unlucky individuals] miss it because they are too focused on looking for something else. Lucky people, on the other hand, are more relaxed and open, which means they see what is there.' Wiseman's study draws on positive psychology. A negative mindset narrows focus, whereas an optimistic positive mindset opens up the field of view. Control is ultimately perception.

There is of course a much darker side to this behaviour of illusionary control. Let's say I'm afraid of flying. I may, over the years, have started and strengthened a routine that involves shutting the front door three times or tapping my hand on the check-in desk to ensure a safe flight. The more I do this and arrive safely, the deeper the neural pathway grows for this pattern of associative thinking and behaviour. My brain double and triple underlines the passage in my filing cabinet that says this behaviour means safety and rewards me neurochemically each time I tap, motivating me to continue. Rationally of course, these actions, as with the athletes and artists above, cannot have any impact on the safety of the flight but it helps me cope and quells my anxiety through repetition – but the behaviour can escalate to become obsessive and all-consuming.

Bias – we can't help ourselves

Another challenge often grappled with in organisations, at both a group and individual level, is bias. Biases are simply another term for the patterns of associations in our files that have been set up to interpret the events and others we encounter. As I've shown, these patterns are our evolved high-speed information processing pathways designed to make efficient decisions with minimal cognitive effort. But while they were and still are hugely beneficial for our survival, these pathways can impede us, limit our view, and blind us to alternative options, leading to unhelpful behaviours and decisions, which can be costly to business. Our brain has only its own internal model of the world to work from and we can easily assume that people think and see the world as we do. We believe our decisions to be right because they come to our conscious selves from the subconscious patterning process otherwise referred to as emotional reasoning. Decisions made on the 'felt sense' of being correct may be based on faulty filing or erroneous information and logic. We tend to distrust, in the first instance, anything different from ourselves and our patterns of thinking because we have created beliefs about situations and others.

There are around 150 academically defined biases. David Rock and Matthew Lieberman have categorised these into four main areas within their COST™ model, basing the ordering on common underlying biology.[98] Here I give you a high-level extract from their paper 'Breaking Bias'.

COST™	Definition	Example Bias
Corner Cutting	Mental shortcuts to help make quick and efficient decisions. Sometimes referred to as the lazy system 1 fact checker – the system that relies on fast, easy associations and intuition.	Availability bias – where we use and consider the most accessible and available information, preventing consideration of broader data. (Tversky & Kahneman,1981)
Objectivism	The conviction to what we perceive as reality. Reality (of one's perception) is black and white, objective.	Blind spot – it is relatively easy to spot a bias in another than in oneself. People rate themselves as less susceptible to biases than others and see their answers as less biased than others. (Pronin et al., 2002)
Self-protection	Focusing on information that gives us significance, puts us in a good light.	Overconfidence bias – we think that we are better than average e.g. driving, leadership, attractiveness. (Von-Veelen & Nowak, 2011)
Time and Money	We are more driven by the negative than by the positive and we place greater value on things that have a greater proximity to us in terms of ownership, space and temporality.	Loss aversion – we take more risks to avoid loss than when in a situation of potential positive gain. (Skowronski & Carlston, 1989) Framing effect – if information is presented or framed as gain people will choose to avoid a risky decision, e.g. they won't take the risky bet for a 60% probability of winning £20. If it is framed as a loss, then people will choose to take the risk more often, e.g. take the risk for the 40% probability of losing £20. (Kahneman & Tervsky,) Temporal discounting – people value things differently depending on whether they get them now or later, e.g. £10 now or £20 later, say a month from now. We devalue or discount the future worth because of its distance or lower tangibility. (Kirby & Marakovic,)

Being right is rewarding, making errors is painful and activates the same region of the brain associated with processing physical pain and negative emotion. Being wrong undermines our sense of reliability with the world. As with any neuronal pattern of thinking, it is hard to first become aware of it. Whilst becoming conscious of your biases is difficult, what is even harder is overcoming and rewiring such thinking. Just making people aware of their biases, usually through simple testing – the most recognised perhaps being the Harvard Implicit Association Test (IAT)[99] – is not enough to mitigate the effects of one's own biases. Intellectual understanding is not the same as behavioural change, which requires neural rewiring. But there are strategies that we can employ in business to mitigate the effect of our biases if we are disciplined enough. Learning from the world of orchestras could help. In the 1970s and 80s orchestras started to use blind auditions even asking candidates to remove their shoes so there was no tell-tale sound of heels to overcome gender bias. Only the music could be heard by the interviewers and led to a surge in the number of women being offered positions. How could this be translated for promotion, recruitment and performance management in your organisation?

I'm right!

Look at these two lines. Are they the same length?

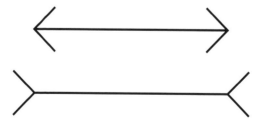

Of course, they are the same length, but as with many optical illusions, even when we consciously know things to be different from how they appear it feels uncomfortable. That sense of being right, referred to by William James as 'felt knowledge' can be a great advantage – such as the doctor instinctively sensing that there is another cause to the illness masked by other symptoms. When we are faced with uncertainty, overwhelming information or face a stressful situation, our capacity to make choices on a purely executive level of cognitive processing diminishes, so we have to call on non-conscious processing to make our decisions. The mental shortcuts we make are often heuristic based on a 'rule of thumb' that allows us to quickly come up with an approximate answer to make sense of a complex, ambiguous environment, often referred to as gut instinct. But these can lead us to draw incorrect conclusions about the situation. These unhelpful errors are cognitive biases. Gut instinct is not by any means foolproof.

Neurobiologist Antonio Damasio's work looks deeper into this cognitive bypass at what he calls Somatic Markers.[100] According to Damasio, every event that we file is connected to a series of bodily sensations that we would have felt when we went through it the first time. When we then encounter a similar event, we re-experience the sensations which send signals for action and guide our decisions – the neuro mechanism for intuition. That sinking feeling, rising heart rate and dry mouth experienced in the presentation that flopped are all somatic markers that when experienced again warn the individual to avoid the situation. Or the trader who trusts in the itch on his right elbow to indicate that it is the right time to buy may ignore rational argument not to invest. In one experiment Damasio asked participants to pick from four decks of cards, which would see them win or lose money. Two decks had smaller wins and losses – between $50 and $100, but over time choosing from these decks would be profitable. The other two decks had higher amounts of win or loss –

between $500 and $1000 – but unlike the first two these decks would culminate in loss. Over time the participants discovered the pattern, but what Damasio showed was that their behaviour changed before they knew the reason or could state what had changed for them. He could identify physical signals: in this case the electrical conductivity of the skin of the participants (which increases with the amount of sweat on the skin) began to spike when they were thinking about the higher risk decks. The sweat was the somatic marker that guided them to the safer decks. Decision making is as much a physical process as it is a mental process.

As we travel through our uncertain world, intuition – our evolutionary shortcut – is highly valuable. It uses the foundations of our experience to guide us. When there is literally no time to think, as in the case of the fire chief, then the instinct to act is the one that can save our lives. In unpredictable and unknown environments, however, there is no baseline file to check against and our somatic markers become less reliable, even completely useless. Daniel Kahneman and Gary Klein identified that for intuition to be more accurate there first needs to be a certain structure to a situation, a certain predictability that allows you to have a basis for the intuition. The second factor is whether decision makers have a chance to get feedback on their judgments so that they can strengthen them and gain expertise. If those criteria aren't met, then intuitions aren't going to be trustworthy.

Kahneman says of intuition, 'You should not take your intuitions at face value. Overconfidence is a powerful source of illusions, primarily determined by the quality and coherence of the story that you can construct, not by its validity. If people can construct a simple and coherent story, they will feel confident regardless of how well grounded it is in reality.'

So, in situations where we do have time, perhaps within a workplace project or strategy evaluation, the key is to be able to listen to our intuition and then bring alongside rational argument and others' views, to challenge what we first believe to be right, to open our mind to other possible options or explanations about our first interpretation. This partnership of the emotional and the rational is the sweet spot of decision making.

What if...

We seek to establish certainty and reliability from the information we receive because with it we can remain in control, taking the right steps to ensure our continued safety. However, the world is not certain and our modern workplaces are anything but. Change is a certainty. Without adaptation, we do not learn but adaptation naturally pushes us outside of our comfort zone. Part of being a leader is to be comfortable with making others uncomfortable so we can develop them and the business. To do this we need the skills to manage the threat that change brings.

What if... when making changes at work we focus only on the one or two that carry the highest value at any one time? Change is threat but also inevitable. We can choose the volume of changes, deliberately keeping as much the same as possible. Moving offices and then using it as a lever to change to new patterns of work won't work but taking one at a time will.

What if... we offset the pain from change by bolstering the sense of belonging and ensuring every individual has a chance and the time to put forward ideas and opinions?

What if... at every stage of a change we keep checking back in with those affected? One organisation that faced a backlash to moving offices finally understood the need to create some sense of certainty.

It did this by taking teams to the new premises to show them where their bank of desks would be, where they could park, even the colour scheme, and despite how simple this may sound it allowed the dissenting brains to establish a picture of what will be and so start to calm.

What if... we strive for consistency in our leadership behaviours? In his book *Speed of Trust* Stephen Covey outlines 13 leadership behaviours for trust. Much of these look at supporting certainty through 'talking straight', 'creating transparency', 'clarifying expectations', 'confronting reality' and 'keeping commitments'. Even if the message is difficult we must deliver it honestly. With knowledge, we can take control.

What if... we clearly lay out the future around any change we need to implement? Our brains can build maps of what is yet to come if we use our imagination to do so. Using methodology to look at what the future may look, sound and feel like brings a picture to our mind's eye, starts to alleviate some of the uncertainty from the unknown and allows us to start to create our memory files of the future. As Stephen Covey says, 'Begin with the end in mind.'

What if... we discipline ourselves to notice our intuitive interpretation? Where we have time, we should create the gap between stimulus and response to bring in rational debate. We can implement cognitive checks to regulate emotional reasoning, particularly when there is environmental unpredictability.

CHAPTER 8

STRETCH

'Satisfaction lies in the effort, not in the attainment, full effort is full victory.'

Mahatma Gandhi

The What...

Learning, growing, change, achieving, striving, winning and losing
– each are a part of life. But why do we play, challenge ourselves
and enter competitions? Why do we get a buzz from winning and
feel pain if defeated? Stretching ourselves is not just taking part in
fun for fun's sake; stretch has a deeper survival benefit. Our habitat
during our evolutionary journey has, in the main, been a harsh
terrain with a constant search for limited resources. It is estimated
that we were designed to walk around 12 miles a day on our hunt for
sustenance. Whilst many millions still live in unforgiving landscapes,
our ancestors' lifestyle was very different from today's western instant
access sedentary lifestyles. You would need to have lived under a stone
to not know that exercise is good for us, but worryingly, sedentary
living is more harmful than smoking and kills more people than HIV.
Sitting is the new smoking! As we sit at our desks, drive to collect our
food and slouch on the sofa watching TV or gaming, we are working
against our physical make-up, increasing our risk of developing several
serious illnesses, such as type 2 diabetes, cancer and heart disease.[101]
We need to move, we need to put in effort for reward and we need to
learn to adapt.

In this chapter I want to explore the reward and benefits of stretch,
play, learning and effort and why these link to intrinsic motivation,
trust and performance.

To win or lose

To win is good. Losing, not so. Failure is painful and can, if we don't
process the defeat effectively, affect our self-esteem and confidence.
The meaning we attribute, and the stories we tell ourselves about
losing, whether it's the race or a bad presentation, will dictate how we
bounce back from it. Termed as attributional or explanatory thinking
styles by psychologists, we can assess how we tend to talk to ourselves
about why things didn't go so well. If you failed a test how would you

tend to look back on it? Would you say to yourself that this is typical of you, this is just your luck and this type of thing happens to you all the time? Or would you say, well it's not what I had wanted but it's a one off, other factors were involved although I'll take responsibility for my share and can learn for the next time?

The first way of thinking is a vulnerable style, while the second is a resilient style. The latter will see you cope, grow and adapt. The first sees you sit with destructive self-blame. We can change our preferred style of thinking through cognitive tools, but why does losing hurt in the first place and why does wining give us such a thrill? Psychology professor Ian Robertson of Trinity College Dublin argues that winning is probably the single most important thing in shaping people's lives. His research shows how, the perhaps obvious link between winning to an individual's place within their social hierarchy, which as we saw in the chapter about Relative Position, has a major impact on our health, mental function and mood. Winning and defeat are chemical interplays within our bodies, which subsequently drive behaviour. Our body language is a clear sign of this chemical reaction. You only have to watch any sporting event and see the behavioural displays of success or loss. Interestingly, coming second is probably the worst place to be, despite it being a great achievement in most circumstances. A study of Olympic athletes looked at how happy medallists appeared and what they found was a common pattern. The gold and bronze medallists were very happy but the silver medallists often showed a blank expression, staring out into the distance. The bronze medallists had just reached the podium, while the silver medallists had just missed the ultimate goal.

A research study from San Francisco State University found that instinctive reaction to victory tended to be nonverbal displays of dominance,[102] such as pumping the chest out, tilting the head back, punching the air, raising the arms above the shoulders, and the face either grimacing or showing aggression or anger. When we are defeated, we do the opposite. We hang our heads, wrap ourselves up, make ourselves smaller and seek to remove ourselves from others – which makes sense if we need to escape from further harm. And, when someone is dominating us, unlike other interactions where we mirror their actions, we can become submissive. As the dominant individuals rise in the social hierarchy, the defeated retreat to the sidelines and lick their wounds, recovering in the hope they might challenge another day. All of which is suggestive of a self-deselection from the evolutionary process supporting Darwin's theory of the survival of the fittest. These bodily reactions are witnessed in animals as well as humans. From an evolutionary psychological perspective, this behaviour is believed to stem from the biological need to establish hierarchy and societal order.

The power-pose

So, using the behaviour associated with winning, can we use physical movement to help us succeed? The social psychologist Amy Cuddy has studied power dynamics and the nonverbal expressions of dominance and power. She brought people into her lab and asked some of them to adopt the types of high power-pose. This involved, for instance, putting their hands on their hips, spreading their feet out wide and puffing their chest out. Others she asked to do the opposite: adopting a low power-pose, head down, shoulders rounded and so on. Before they took the stance, she tested their spit for certain hormonal levels. After two minutes she asked the power-posers, 'How powerful do you feel?' and then gave them the opportunity to gamble. The results showed that 86% of those who were in the high power-pose chose to gamble, while only 60% of the low power-poses did so. From a hormonal aspect those high power-posers experienced around a 20% increase in testosterone from the base level and the low power-pose had a 10% decrease. For cortisol, the stress hormone, the high power-posers had a 25% decrease and for the low power-posers a 15% increase. Cuddy's work shows that our bodies can influence the chemical levels that configure the brain. In just two minutes we can change our minds to be more, or less, confident and assertive. As we grow in confidence we take more risks, grasp more opportunities and gain more success.

So What?

The agony of losing

Part of the pain of losing is the decrease in testosterone and the release of norepinephrine, which has a regulatory effect on negative emotions. The amygdala, primarily active during experiences of emotions such as fear, anger and sadness, receives signals from norepinephrine, influencing the agony of defeat. Winning, on the other hand, increases testosterone in both men and women but it also increases dopamine. It is this latter chemical messenger that taps into the reward network in the brain, which is the feel-good factor we get from achieving a goal, accomplishing a task, or winning the competition. These positive chemical boosts have an impact on our longevity. So as the health impact and the social ordering effect of winning are rewarded we become more motivated to perform and engage. The case is no different at work. Winning the pitch, a successful negotiation, gaining market share or experiencing the sale all provide the same effect. Recognising and noticing achievement, no matter how small, amplifies the sense of reward. Dopamine has many properties, one of which is increased activity in the frontal lobes. This influences better decision making and connectivity of information. We so often focus on the things that have not gone so well, pushing the small wins we get each day to one side. Instead of increasing engagement, this concentration on what's wrong is demoralising and has the opposite effect to performance and innovation. I'll talk more about this later in the chapter when I discuss giving feedback.

The winning and losing impact is not just an individual reaction. It extends beyond those taking part to those witnessing the event. Think back to when you last watched a sporting event where you were rooting for a player or team – how did you feel as the game played out and your competitor found themselves winning or losing? The chemicals in your brain would have been changing as you sat biting your nails on the edge of your seat.

On the night of the 2008 American Presidential elections, one study found that testosterone levels of male Obama voters stayed level whereas the testosterone level of the McCain and Barr voters dropped.[103] Scientists at Princeton University's Neuroscience Institute have investigated this contagion effect. They are leading the way in measuring how the perceptual experience of one brain can impact the motor system of another, termed brain-to-brain coupling. For example, a national crowd cheering you on and being positive matched with the power of your intention and effort is a potentially measurable phenomenon. If the scientists have it right, it means that an athlete or individual being cheered is likely to achieve a higher result than could have been achieved in isolation. If you've ever run a 5K or 10K race you'll understand the powerful influence of the crowd on your motivation and ability to continue. From a survival aspect, this makes sense to me. If we support our home team, our tribe or community we increase our group's chances of survival over competition for limited resources. No different for rooting for our team at work and our organisation. An individual success should always be measured in terms of the team's success. One win, all win.

Just the right amount of stretch

But winning or losing is the result, not the whole story. For many situations, the outcome is preceded by huge effort, sometimes over long periods of time. Effort is, in and of itself, rewarding. If it weren't, we wouldn't have survived on the African savannahs where obtaining food was a full-time occupation. Neither would we ever continue in the face of anything that looked like hard work. We need to be motivated to keep going.

In 1908, the Yerkes-Dodson law was published, describing the non-linear relationship between mental arousal and performance.[104] The study was an analysis of the influence of the difficulty and stress of a learning-based task on mice. The paper was published without any statistical analysis (because statistical analyses didn't yet exist) and with unacceptably small sample sizes compared to today's standards, but it remains as a powerful influence on cognitive psychology and research because of what the study inadvertently found. Their study found when mice were given a simple task their performance improved linearly with increases in pressure arousal. With the performance of more difficult tasks, they improved under moderate increases in pressure until a tipping point, where highest levels of pressure started to diminish performance. The result formed a non-linear, inverted U-shaped relationship between levels of pressure and performance. What they had been unknowingly tracking at the time was the circuitry that secretes stress hormones when the amygdala is activated. They showed that under-stretch leads to boredom and disengagement. As the pressure rises there are incremental improvements in performance until we achieve optimal performance. Then performance declines as the pressure overloads the system leading to distress.

Since its publication, the Yerkes-Dodson law has led to decades of research into why performance can be either improved or diminished when participants face increasing levels of stress or pressure (arousal). What the ensuing research has shown is that the ultimate shape of the curve is dependent on variables such as the nature of the task or the environmental influences.[105]

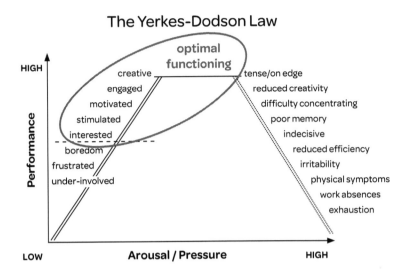

The Yerkes-Dodson Law

What all of this is saying is that we need a certain level of pressure or stress to motivate ourselves to action. Without it boredom sets in: those mundane tasks that seem so painful to even start, the experience of time dragging its heels with every minute feeling like an hour. With the right levels of stretch, pressure and purpose, we are motivated to a point of optimal performance – that sensation of time flying, sometimes referred to as Eustress (Eu the Greek prefix meaning good).[106] This links to the work of Mihaly Csikszentmihalyi, professor of psychology and management at Claremont University. In his work on the psychology of optimal performance he describes the state of Flow[107] as a balance between the challenge of the task and the skill of the performer, where we are completely immersed in the task and have complete concentration. Here we meet deadlines, have maximum cognitive efficiency, the flexibility to respond to shifting challenges, reach goals and use our talents optimally – all of which feels pleasurable. Too much stretch leaves us overwhelmed, dissipating our perception of control and switches on the threat circuitry. If we are under or overstretched, performance drops, cognition is depleted and if this state of play continues the body reacts by producing greater levels of the stress hormone cortisol. Cortisol has both beneficial and harmful effects. In short, acute periods of stress increased cortisol, alongside adrenaline and dopamine, extends our alertness and capacity to carry out tasks. As the period of stress lengthens and becomes chronic the impact of cortisol becomes harmful, technically called allostatic load, creating imbalances in our immune and nervous systems leaving us more vulnerable to disease.

Cortisol is a catabolic steroid hormone, meaning it breaks things down. Long-term exposure to cortisol damages our hippocampus, the seat of learning where short-term memories are converted to long term. The hippocampus is rich in receptors for cortisol due to its part in memory formation, but too much cortisol will impair memory retrieval and learning and can cause memory loss. Repeated stressful events or one continual source of stress, such as an abrasive boss, uncontrollable workload, unachievable targets or expectations beyond our skill or knowledge, will all take their toll on our physiology. In the majority of organisations I've worked with, the signs of overstretch incubation are apparent but this is often accepted as 'just the way work is'. This is a dangerous de-sensitisation that not only affects employee performance but also our economy, with implications for society, community and our health.

The right levels of stretch for growth and motivation need to be understood and assessed properly. Too little, boredom and complacency sets in; too much is the path for collapse. Several years ago, I had a conversation with a friend of my father whose son was a foreign exchange trader – and a very successful one at that. He told me about the time he asked his son why he appeared manic for the first couple of weeks of the month and then less busy towards the end. His son explained that in most months he hit his target within the first couple of weeks and then worked until he reached the extra 10% that ensured his bonus. His father asked why he didn't continue to work as hard to achieve even more each month. The reply was, 'Why? I don't get any more.' In this case the target had unintentionally diminished performance, albeit going under the radar since achievement was at 110%. Targets are motivational and drive performance as long as they represent, as Goldilocks would say, just the right amount of stretch. Any goal that is unrealistic only serves to demotivate.

Effort and the IKEA effect

This brings me to effort in its purest sense. Have you ever tried to put together a flat pack piece of furniture? It's a frustrating process. The likelihood is that these pieces are not the most expensive you own or will own but they are treasured because you built them. Your frustration, sweat and maybe even tears went into creating the slightly wobbly structure. This is pride from effort and an emotional reward is triggered each time we recognise that achievement. Dan Ariely, professor of psychology and behavioural economics at Duke University, called this the IKEA effect. As part of his research he studies effort and its impact on motivation. In one experiment, he gave origami novices instructions and paper to fold into a relatively ugly form. He then asked each of them how much they would pay for their work and asked the same question of those who had watched the work. He then ran the same experiment but this time didn't provide the instructions. The result was a harder test and an even uglier product. In the first experiment, the origami creators said they would pay around five times more than those that had simply watched them build. In the second experiment this gap was exaggerated, with the builders valuing the even uglier products of their labour higher while the observers dropped their valuation. The value we place on our work is directly aligned to the effort we put in and we expect others to value it in the same way.

Now imagine you have created a report that you took time over and poured effort into. With pride, you hand the report to your boss who does not look at it and drops it on a pile without comment. A short while after, you get the report back on your desk, covered in red ink with corrections. How do you feel? Now if we rewind: you hand in the report and your boss looks at it, thanks you and remarks that she can see the effort you have taken. She says that she will read it through over the next couple of days and get back to you with her thoughts for discussion. Instead of getting the report back with passive-aggressive red scribbles all over it, your boss asks you to pop in. She again remarks on the effort you have taken. She runs through some thoughts she has to make it even stronger. How do you feel now? In the very first stage of my career I worked for a boss who loved his red pen, wielding it like a sword of domination. The markings he left in his path dismissed genuine effort and heads hung low on the receipt of every slashed report. Whether intentional or unintentional, unnoticed effort damages motivation and engagement.

Going back to Dan Ariely's work, he gave students at MIT a piece of paper filled with random letters, and asked them to find pairs of identical letters. Each round, they were offered less money than the previous round. People in the first group wrote their names on their sheets and handed them to the experimenter, who looked it over and said, 'Uh huh' before putting it on a pile. People in the second group didn't write down their names, and the experimenter put their sheets on a pile without looking at them. People in the third group had their work shredded immediately upon completion. People whose work was shredded needed to be given double the amount of money to keep doing the task as those whose work was acknowledged. People in the second group, whose work was saved but ignored, needed almost as much money as those whose work was shredded. 'Ignoring the performance of people is almost as bad as shredding their effort before their eyes,' Ariely says. 'The good news is that adding motivation doesn't seem to be so difficult. The bad news is that eliminating motivation seems to be incredibly easy.'

In his TED talk, Ariely tells us of the lessons learnt from the introduction of cake mix. In the 1950s, instant cake mix was introduced as part of initiatives to simplify the American housewife's manual load. The cake mixes were immediately resisted by their intended audience. They made cooking all too easy and, from their perspective, undervalued their work. So, the manufacturers took them off the shelves and replaced them with a mix that required them to add an egg. As the saying goes, the mixes flew off the shelves like hot cakes (couldn't resist that one!) and they remain on our supermarket shelves today, saving parents from the shame of the 'not baked at home' offering at the school fair (me included). What this is all telling us is that effort increases our valuation of the work and the joy of the final product. In the workplace, acknowledging effort is vital, as is providing the opportunity to own the effort expended. Celebrate the output but place a focus on rewarding the input of effort.

Building on the reward of effort brings me to the important work of Carol Dweck, professor of psychology at Stanford University. In the late 1960s Dweck was studying animal motivation, which included learned helplessness. She started to question how humans cope with situations that left us feeling powerless and why some capable children gave up in the face of failure while others may be motivated to continue. Dweck posited that this related to people's belief about why they had failed. Those who attributed a lack of ability to the failure would avoid or give up but those who thought that with greater effort they could achieve would persevere. This idea led to her PhD dissertation. She ran an experiment with young schoolchildren that had been identified by the school as helpless. When these children, for example, faced mathematical problems they couldn't solve, it led them to give up, which subsequently made them unable to solve mathematical challenges that they had previously been able to. Through several exercises, half the children were encouraged to put their errors down to lack of effort and supported to keep going. The other half – the control group – were given no intervention. Those who learned to persist found themselves succeeding whilst the control group remained the same, falling apart in the face of problems and slowly recovering.

What Dweck was doing was putting the attributional theory I've mentioned previously into practical use to help change mindsets. She continued her research after this initial study, instructing the children she worked with to see failure as information and as a challenge to be solved. She also positioned goals around learning rather than performance – an important difference and one we can take on board in the workplace. This insight led to a new field of educational psychology – achievement goal theory. Dweck started to see that children who were told they were clever would often perform tasks that let them look smart even if it meant not learning anything, while avoiding other challenges that they did not, as yet, have the capability to succeed in. This led her to the theory of fixed and growth mindsets. A fixed mindset assumes that intelligence is set in stone and unchangeable while those with a growth mindset believe intelligence can be developed.

Dweck tells her own story of when she was a child and how her teacher, a Mrs Wilson, organised her and her classmates in order of IQ, which, hopefully unintentionally, displayed a fixed mindset to the children. While Dweck says this didn't scar her as she already had some of the growth mindset, she has shown that a fixed mindset creates a real ceiling to learning and potential. Her work shows that by shifting the self-beliefs of low-achieving schoolchildren regarding their ability to learn, rewarding their effort supports them to achieve remarkable results. Of this, Dweck says, 'Study skills and learning skills are inert until they're powered by an active ingredient. Students may know how to study but won't want to if they believe their efforts are futile. If you target that belief, you can see more benefit than you have any reason to hope for.'

Dweck also is clear in saying that we all have different abilities and are naturally more or less able at some things, but her evidence shows that if we hold a fixed mindset we simply won't reach as high as we might be able to. Effort is vital for anything we wish to achieve, so issues arise when we believe that effort on any task, even a hard one, implies low ability. Many schools are starting to use Dweck's research in the classroom, but it is equally applicable in the workplace, where a fixed mindset is systemically perpetuated via performance targets, appraisal processes and ineffective feedback. The appraisal system in many organisations needs, quite simply, to be thrown out with the recycling. Any process that boxes an individual in a rating runs the risk of fixing their mindset to a level of capability. The predetermined distribution bell curve – where 80% of employees are to sit in the middle – flies in the face of growth and learning.

I have led many teams. Every time I was expected to fit the mould of performance rating results, I complained. I explained that the potential we have needs to be supported to continue to develop without constraints forced on them by closed metrics. These metrics were not designed for development but to control and to neatly feed into financial budget calculations for salary and bonus pools. I didn't win back then, but there are organisations now that are dramatically changing the way they support growth. They are removing the mandatory ranking systems that take up inordinate amounts of time for HR, employees and managers, and are instead focusing on strengths, learning and the quality of continual conversations that are truly motivational because every interaction works with our own reward mechanism.

Carol Dweck worked with Albert Bandura, whose work on self-efficacy refers to an individual's belief in his or her capacity to execute behaviours necessary to produce specific performance attainments *(Bandura, 1977, 1986, 1997)*, as well as their confidence to exert control over their motivation and the environment. Bandura frames the conception of ability. He tested the idea that one's view of ability affects thought processes and performance attainment on participants carrying out management tasks. With a group of managers, Bandura and his colleague instilled the idea that managerial tasks within the simulated organisation reflected inherent intellectual capacity. Another group of managers were told that their performance on the tasks reflected an acquirable intellectual skill. For the first set of managers their efficacy dropped as they came up against problems, they lowered the aspirations for the group they managed, their analytical thinking became more erratic, and performance deteriorated. But those that had been told that the skills were acquirable fostered a highly resilient sense of personal efficacy and remained committed to the task despite the challenges, continued setting goals for their group, and were effective in the analytical assessment.[108] As we strive for goals and learning we will make mistakes; in fact without error there is no progression, only repetition of what we already know and can do. From time to time we should receive social comparison so we can judge our progress, but for this to be effective it is not forced upon us in any pre-defined matrix. Building a growth mindset that supports self-efficacy, focusing on skills as acquirable, and moving away from forced social comparison and ranking, will tap into intrinsic reward and support learning.

Talent or effort?

Alongside effort lies practice. Practice makes perfect, as the saying goes, and certainly practice is key to success and learning. Research carried out in the late 1990s by Anders Ericsson, professor of psychology at Florida State University, showed how those in society who are seen as having extraordinary talents were actually the product of deliberate practice and stretching effort. They targeted areas for improvement, rather than simply believing themselves to be in possession of some innate gift of talent. That is not to say there aren't physical advantages: height for example is a clear advantage in basketball. Ericsson's study looked at musicians and showed that those who excelled had simply practised more, usually extended across ten years or the much-cited 10,000 hours. Crucially they also deliberately built in time for rest. We are not designed to keep going at full pelt, we must take time for renewal. Sports players of course know this well and their training regimes are developed to incorporate rejuvenation.

It is no different for the workplace. Our cognitive resources are energy hungry and the more complex and unknown the task, the quicker the fuel is used. Ever had that time when you have read the same line in a book twice, thrice? Realised that your mind is wandering? When you notice this, take some time out. Your cognitive juices are running on empty but with a short break they can quickly be replenished. Mindfulness or a stretch of the legs will allow you to refuel the cognitive tank. Ignoring this natural ebb and flow of our cognitive energy gives rise to diminishing returns. If we have not taken time to re-energise, cognitive fatigue across the day depletes our decision making and executive function, slows performance and injects risk both for the organisation and our own health. Taking breaks, however, remains often counter-intuitive and counter-cultural.

Talent is not some magical power or special miracle you are born with but something that is developed through effort and practice. In Matthew Syed's brilliant book *Bounce*, he provides many examples that debunk the myth of talent and provide the answers to achievement through opportunity and practice. His own story, as he writes, is a case in point. His first opportunity came when his parents bought him and his brother a full-size table tennis table and put it up in the garage, following which he and his brother spent hours playing. Soon after, the Omega table tennis club was set up by Peter Charters, the nation's top coach at the time and a senior figure in the English Table Tennis Association. He invited Syed and his brother to join, as he did others from the same neighbourhood, giving them all opportunity and space to practise, supported by a hugely motivating and dedicated coach. The club was open 24 hours a day and all the children had keys. Syed went on to be the English number one for many years, three times Commonwealth Gold Champion and twice an Olympian. His brother went on to become one of the most successful junior players of all time, winning three national titles.

Syed tells us about the results of this opportunity and practice. The Syeds lived at 119, and at number 274 lived Karen Witt who became one of the most brilliant female players of her generation, gaining prestigious prizes including the Commonwealth Championship. At 149 was Andy Wellman, another leading player, and then at the bottom of the road Keith Holder (outstanding county player); around the corner Jimmy Stokes (England junior champion); Paul Savins (junior international); Alison Gordon (four times English senior champion), and he could go on, he says. Syed writes: *'For a period in the 1980s, this one street, and the surrounding vicinity, produced more outstanding table tennis players than the rest of the nation combined... a ping-pong mecca that seemed to defy explanation or belief.'* And if this doesn't convince you, perhaps the next story will.

Forty-five years ago, Laszlo Polgar, a Hungarian psychologist, courted a Ukrainian teacher called Klara. The union was not one of great love or romance, instead he and Klara married to carry out probably one of the most extreme pedagogical experiments of all time. Polgar believed that he could turn any healthy child into a prodigy through early and intensive effortful practice and specialism in a chosen field. He chose chess as the game through which his theory could be proved. He and Klara had three daughters, and when the eldest was only four years old Polgar started to teach her, and later the other two siblings, chess. Chess was the perfect game because it provided measurable results over time and combined both art and science. They practised for hours every day and at the age of 16, Susan, the eldest, dominated the New York Open chess competition. At the same competition, the middle daughter Sophia won most of her games in her section and the youngest, Judit, showed her amazing ability by playing five matches at once and winning them all – blindfolded! Susan went on to be the first female grand master at the age of 21, the same title awarded to Judit in the same year at only 15.

The reward of learning

The type of dedication needed to achieve mastery is a drive that is not often seen. In fact, it is the 'desire to master' that fuels continued practice and provides the reward to the individual. Dweck says of Laszlo that he provided an environment where failure was inevitable and by keeping them focused on the learning goal he probably protected them from seeing their chess ability as a 'precious gift they would sit and polish'. For most of us, perhaps the opportunity to specialise and practise never materialised or we chose to vary our activities becoming a master of none. Whatever our own circumstances the natural reward from learning, building our competence, is one that we all have.

Effort and learning are needed for our survival. If we had never adapted, increased our knowledge, or added to our skills, we would not have raced up the evolutionary tree as we have. Curiosity seems to be a key. If we are interested in a subject and know a little about it but are faced with a gap in our knowledge our curiosity drives us to know more and extend our ability. Research carried out at the University of California showed that when people were more curious, brain activity rose in regions known to transmit dopamine.[109] Dopamine appears to have a critical part to play in how and why we learn and are motivated to continue to do so. Scientists have shown in animals that when dopamine release is blocked they become less interested in engaging in pleasurable activities such as eating. Rats with lesions to the brain areas responsible for dopamine will starve to death if not force-fed. They are still physically able to eat but lose all interest in doing so.

The emerging theory is that dopamine acts as a teaching tool. The timing of its release appears to provide the signal that something will be pleasurable and thus motivate us to engage. If the results are good then more dopamine is produced to teach us to continue engaging or, if it turns out to be bad, then dopamine levels drop and we move away.[110] While it remains controversial, this research does provide a very plausible logic explaining how and why we are motivated to learn, while also illustrating how learning is a necessary part of that survival process, supported by the pleasure chemical dopamine. Learning represents potential for growth and adaptation, and dopamine acts as the 'save as' request in the brain, locking attention on to useful information.

Let's play

So far in this chapter I have spoken about the chemical reward of winning, the joy of effort, the success obtained through deliberate practice and the reward from learning. But there is one more important element to the area of stretch: play. Play is taking part in an activity for no other purpose than the joy it brings... but is it just this? Why is play rewarding? If reward is delivered to us because we are involved in something that brings us survival benefits, what other properties might play have?

In 1966, Charles Whitman of Austin, Texas, a veteran marine sniper, stabbed, shot and killed his mother and his wife. He then climbed the observation tower of the University of Texas and rained terror down on the people below. In a rampage that lasted just under two hours, 16 people lost their lives and many more were injured before police killed him. At the same time, Stuart Brown was studying the psychology of aggression and heard the news report of Whitman's shooting frenzy live. Following the tragedy, Brown's boss suggested that he study Whitman, so he followed what was to be a life-long study into play. Why play? Brown reconstructed Whitman's life in a great deal of detail. There were of course several factors to Whitman's life experience, including a violent father who beat him and his mother relentlessly, but when Brown interviewed Whitman's teachers and childhood neighbours something else stood out. Whitman's father would punish him severely any time he attempted any type of free play. The neighbours said that they did not remember Whitman ever playing, and his teachers said that he was 'too good', sitting in the classroom waiting for instruction on what to do rather than taking part in the normal anarchic play of boys of his age. This lack of play during his early age appeared to be salient, but Whitman was only one subject.

So Brown started to explore this further. He went to Huntsville prison, a place nicknamed 'Walls Unit' (because of the 15-foot-high brick wall that surrounds it) that houses the Texas state execution chamber, the most active chamber in the United States. It has held some of the most notorious and dangerous criminals; there Brown interviewed 26 murderers. In every case the same story played out. The lack of rough and tumble play and the subjects' lack of empathy appeared to be linked. Experience of play where you push another and learn the impact of creating and feeling pain – and vice versa – supports the development of empathy. In a state of play we take more risks and so learn, often painfully, what is safe and what our limitations are whilst at the same time growing our capability. We learn how we can trust others and the 'rules' of social interaction.

Brown has continued his research, setting up the National Institute for Play. Studies looked at how the lack of play, particularly during our very early years, has a damaging effect on the brain. Brown stresses that play is important at any age. When you are in a state of play, part of your frontal lobe opens and a lot more associations occur; in his words: 'the brain joins up like a symphony'. Play lights up the brain like nothing else: we make new connections, new maps and get mood uplift. The opposite of play is not work, it is depression. Think about life without play, imagination, games, festivals…

There is also a lot of evidence about play from the animal world. Rats are hard-wired to play at a certain point in their development. If you take this away from them and then present them with a cat-saturated collar, those that had been left to play normally flee and then begin to explore a new environment, but the non-players stay where they are, which in the wild would result in death. This suggests that play allows us to learn, adapt, and explore our capabilities and limitations. Isabel Behnke is a primatologist. In her research of bonobos, she watched how they, at all ages, play – albeit to a lesser extent as they age. She questioned what play provided, proposing that perhaps it is not frivolous but essential to their survival. She followed the bonobo communities for over three thousand kilometres of the Congo jungle. She observed the link between trust, ambiguity and risk taking to play. As she watched older bonobos holding the arm of younger ones, reaching beyond the branch of the tree they were sitting on, she could see how they learned to trust each other. She also showed that play is a social connector – glue for the group; through positive emotion, trust spreads through them all.

She has taken her research to human behaviour, studying people at Burning Man festival – an annual week-long festival of free expression in Nevada's Black Rock Desert. People engage with people they didn't know before, take risks, push their limits and lower their inhibitions. She says, 'We share a common root for play. Our reward system in our brains is overdeveloped so obviously we have a capacity for positive emotion and joy that has been an important drive in our evolution. You see live expressions of these roots in normal human behaviour, anything from expression in fashion to competitive sports to literature. Of course, that's where you suspend your belief and you go into these fictional worlds quite happily because that's what play does. It suspends reality. Things that don't usually happen can happen. So we train our brain to explore all these different worlds safely… Play is not just child's games. For us and them, play is foundational for building relationships and fostering tolerance. It's where we learn to trust and where we learn about the rules of the game. Play increases creativity and resilience, and it's all about the generation of diversity – diversity of interactions, diversity of behaviours, diversity of connections.'

The link of play to empathy has also been demonstrated through an interesting experiment involving ice-cold water and strangers. We are not naturally wired to extend empathy to a stranger; in fact, our initial reaction is to assess someone we don't know for potential threat. We evolved living in groups of around 100 to 150 people where no one was a stranger, so we are evolutionarily suspicious. The threat of someone unknown forms a heightened level of stress, which depletes empathy. Jeff Mogil, neuroscientist and senior author at McGill University, Montreal, Canada, showed that if you put two strangers into a room their heart rates – stress levels – increased even though they weren't doing anything. He then ran an experiment. He took two people who did not know each other and got them to plunge their hands into icy cold water for 30 seconds, and then immediately after they took their hands out, he asked them to rate their pain and how much pain they thought the other person was feeling. He ran this same experiment with the participants on their own, once with a stranger and then one more time, but this time with a friend. When participants were tested across from their friends they reported their pain as higher than when they were tested on their own or with a stranger.

The explanation here is that your pain increases with the addition of your friend's pain. This form of empathy is called emotional contagion. The stranger's pain doesn't affect you as much because the stress aroused acts as a dimmer switch for our empathy system. From a survival perspective, it's better to stay emotionally disconnected from a potential foe in case of conflict. Think about how you feel when you hear bad news about someone you don't know versus a friend telling you something upsetting about them. Mogil has, however, found that this stress can be reduced quickly through play that taps into our empathy circuits. If two strangers, for example, play Rock Band (a game where each player has a controller modelled in the form of an instrument and via a video game you then simulate the performance of popular rock music) for 15 minutes. Afterwards the strangers show the same level of stress and empathy as one would for a friend.[111] Play connects us.

The capacity to play allows us to take in novelty and adapt. Play creates a sense of safety within which we feel comfortable to embrace uncertainty and ambiguity that we otherwise wouldn't. Play is rewarding because it supports our survival, stretching us to achieve new heights. The question therefore is how can we bring this state effectively into the boardroom and teams to build our capacity for innovation? One idea that is gaining credence is the use of technology through gaming.

Jane McGonigal, a games designer, is trying to show the positive power of gaming. After gaining a PhD in performance studies, she started developing her first commercial games. Her research focuses on how games are transforming the way we lead our real lives, and how they can be used to increase our resilience and wellbeing. In 2009, she suffered a concussion that did not heal properly, leaving her with debilitating symptoms including continual headaches. Her doctor told her that she needed to avoid anything that would exacerbate her symptoms. No reading, watching television, writing, caffeine, alcohol and so on. Suicidal ideation occurred as her brain started to tell her that her pain would never end and there was no reason to stay alive. From her work, she knew that when we tackle a problem with a game we approach it with more optimism, creativity, and are more likely to reach out to others for help. So, she created a role-playing game in which she was Jane the concussion slayer. She played with her husband and her twin sister and together they identified the bad guys, meaning anything that could trigger her symptoms and therefore slow down her recovery. They also collected 'power-ups' – anything that could make her feel a little better even on her worst day: things like cuddling her dog, or getting out of bed and walking around the block just once. It wasn't a video game, just a gamified way to tackle her pain.

After just a few days the suicidal thoughts disappeared. It wasn't a cure for the symptoms but, as she says, even when she was in pain she stopped suffering. From her experience, she designed the online game SuperBetter, a computer-based game where individuals become their own secret identity, recruiting their own allies, and adopting power-ups to tackle things such as cancer, chronic pain and depression. The game has helped over half a million individuals tackle real life challenges. McGonigal is clear in saying that games should not and cannot be used to motivate anyone to do something they don't want to, instead believing games can be a powerful source through which collective intelligence can be enhanced and human life improved. For me, McGonigal is using technology to harness what we are built to do – that is to use play to tap into our biological reward mechanism for stretch, learning and adaptation.

Feedback

'Can I give you some feedback?' An often rhetorical sentence used thousands of times across many workplaces that can instantly trigger a threat response. We can respond differently to these words depending on our mood, the situation, the person providing the feedback and so on, but under any circumstance they remain emotive, often placing us in a position of lowered status because the other person is effectively saying that there is a problem. After all, we don't ask permission to deliver good news! Have you ever had an appraisal where, despite many positives, you've come away holding on to the one negative that may have only been 2% of the total conversation? And that 2%

spirals around and around in your mind, sometimes for days. When delivered well, feedback is a valuable part of learning but it remains a source of angst for managers, particularly around tackling the things that didn't go so well. If we work with our biology, understanding how we learn and what allows us to grow, we can access ways of providing feedback that really supports potential rather than restricting it.

I am regularly asked, often with a sense of desperation, about how to give feedback. Feedback is an age-old challenge that is laid at the feet of managers, who carry out the task with varying degrees of success. There are many models out there that describe how to give feedback but what most fail to take into account is how the brain reacts and how we really learn. Feedback that triggers our neurological reward circuitry and which increases our capacity for learning and engagement is possible. My work on intrinsic motivation has led me to build and now teach a brain-friendly model for feedback which I'd like to share with you. It is a simple checklist for positive conversations that lead to development not demotivation – and it's as simple as AEIOU.

A – And. If I said to you, 'That presentation was great...' what word are you expecting to hear next? 'But' or 'However'? Now what happens to the words that preceded the 'but'? Our brains home in on threat, which in this case is the criticism that is anticipated to follow. As our brain waits for the bad news it deletes the positives. So, instead of 'but' or 'however' use 'and'. This will feel awkward at first but it works. 'That presentation was great, *and* to make it even stronger you could...' It is not about ignoring what went wrong. The facts are the facts and should be acknowledged and we can deliver the tough stuff with respect.

E – Effort. When we see a baby taking his/her first steps followed promptly by a fall, do we focus on what went wrong and ignore the first step? No, we praise the effort, the accomplishment and focus on supporting step number two. And yet in the workplace we most often place attention on what's not achieved or what's wrong rather than the effort, the strengths, and aspects that have gone well. Focusing on the negative emphasises what's wrong and undermines motivation, ironically reducing performance. Research shows that we are intrinsically rewarded for our effort, so let's praise it more and do so regularly. After all, you wouldn't wait for the annual appraisal to deliver feedback to the baby learning to walk!

I – Intention. People come to work to do a good job. So first think what their intention was before an error occurred. Was it to cause harm, to damage, to destroy? There is an impact which needs to be addressed but first understand the intention.

O – Opportunity. Focus on the power of yet, a growth mindset and opportunity to develop. In addition to effort we can enhance self-efficacy by validating that skills are acquirable. In every genuine error there is an opportunity to learn. Mistakes are part of life. If we didn't make mistakes we would never learn or adapt. That's not to say that we don't need to mitigate the risk of potential mistakes. Of course we do, but we also need to understand how to provide developmental input that really works. The aviation industry has long encouraged all staff, including pilots, to submit every mistake and adverse incident without fear of reprisal. The learning this industry gets every single day is priceless.

U – You. How are you feeling? What are you thinking? What is your mood? What messages are you transmitting that will either help or hinder the conversation? Is this the right time to talk?

Positive development and growth of those in your team happens when our brains can engage and that happens only when we feel safe to do so. Applying AEIOU is a tool to help do this.

One last point, development is not an annual event. It needs to happen every day and in the moment if it is to make the best connections for learning.

What if...

What if... we bring play and gamification to strategy and tactic meetings? How could our avatars help us envision and play out different futures? Not so strange when you think of what the film industry and online gaming already do.

What if... we ripped up the performance bell curve, box-rating systems, league tables and arduous performance appraisal processes? None of these systems accurately reflect human performance and all undermine motivation. And all leave managers with agonising decisions as they try to force-fit their teams, inadvertently curbing performance. Continual conversation that stimulates reward, enhances learning and engenders trust is what we need. Let's start from the premise that the adults you have recruited want to do a good job and we don't know, given the right environment, what their potential may be.

What if... we replaced performance targets with learning goals? The first is a ceiling, the latter is growth.

What if... we recognised under and overstretch and addressed the balance? Doing more with less is a short-term tactic that destroys longer term performance and value. Challenge is great and in a brain-safe environment people will keep growing, naturally able to take on more.

What if... we built into our day space for cognitive renewal? Cognitive advantage is competitive advantage but we need to work with our natural energy flow. There are many organisations offering sleep pods and other breakout spaces, which is fantastic, but to really allow a shift in how we manage our energy a change needs to be underpinned by cultural acceptance and social norms.

What if... we supported leaders to understand and be able to deliver the AEIOU of learning? Focusing on a growth mindset that boosts self-efficacy. We need to give space to practise and space to fail (intelligently and fast). 'Learn to fail or fail to learn' is not a well-known quote for nothing.

CHAPTER 9
AND FINALLY

'The only journey is the one within.'

Rainer Maria Rilke

Identifying the DRIVERS

The DRIVERS can be used as a checklist to help build self-awareness, emotional literacy, interpret and understand others' behaviours, and to inform engagement, change and performance strategies across all activities that involve human beings – so that's everything then!

A first step is to apply them for yourself. Think back to when you experienced a change. How did you think, feel and how did you behave at work and at home? What DRIVERS were being supported or quashed for you? What about the last tricky conversation you had. Did you feel your opinions were not taken seriously, threatening your sense of position relative to the other person? How did you react? Or perhaps you can think of that controlling boss who gave you little choice over how you approached work and was constantly clock-watching everyone. What did you think about him/her and how did this make you feel? How was your performance affected?

You can run through the DRIVERS to assess what is happening against each one when you face both difficult situations and positive experiences. During challenge they help to uncover why you feel and want to react the way that you do. The DRIVERS give you the reason behind the emotions providing you with a chance to target what is wrong. Equally, when things are going well notice which are being supported and how that makes you feel. How can you continue to reinforce the DRIVERS positively?

Where are your DRIVERS?

Take a moment to think about your DRIVERS in different aspects of your life. Overall are they being supported or threatened in the following environments?

- Your role

- Your team

- Your organisation

- Your life

On the lines below mark and annotate a position for each of the DRIVERS where 0 is completely quashed with gradients of greater satisfaction up to 10 where they are fully supported. I have put an example here:

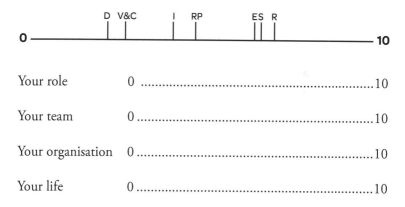

Your role   0 10

Your team   0 10

Your organisation   0 10

Your life   0 10

What you have now is a picture of where each of the DRIVERS sits for you in relation to each other within different environments. Which would you like to move closer to 10? What are your options? What is in your influence to change to enhance them? What are the tweaks that you could make to effect a positive change? With those further away from 10 than you like, how is this affecting you – mild irritation or deeper anxiety? How much of your attention each day is taken to thinking about those you'd like to enhance? How does it feel noticing those DRIVERS that are close to 10?

You can use this exercise with others and with your team to help them understand what may be going on for their DRIVERS, allowing them to target action and positive change.

The DRIVERS for others

Have a look at these scenarios and see if you can spot the DRIVERS under threat.

Clare sat stoically although you could sense her frustration. 'I'm sorry,' she said, 'they have decided not to go ahead with the project. I don't know why but perhaps there's a good reason. Anyway, until we hear more from them we'll put aside the work we've prepared and get on with business as usual.'

*

Gareth had been asked to carry out a feasibility study on the proposed office sale. He had spent time researching and writing the analysis. A day before the agreed deadline Gareth walked confidently into his manager Susan's office and handed over the finished report. Susan lifted her head to greet him, took the report, placed it to one side on her desk without a glance at it and said, 'Oh, yes thanks Gareth. Looks like we'll not be going ahead on things now after all.'

*

Sarah sat at her desk and looked around her. It was gone 6pm and most heads were still down working diligently on whatever needed to be done. Today, like the last few days, had crawled by at a snail's pace. Trying to give the illusion of being busy was draining and the work she had been told to do was not taxing and really didn't take her all day, and what was the point of the work? It just seemed to be replicating data from one screen to another. How long should she sit here – could she leave now? Would that be seen as too early?

*

Applying the DRIVERS to day-to-day conversations and events will help you to notice that people tell you what is wrong or right with their DRIVERS even if they are not aware of it themselves. From there, even if you can't relate to why they are holding the perception they do, you can start to target the solution. Ask them direct and closed questions to verify what you think you are hearing: 'Does this seem unfair to you?' 'Do you feel included?' 'Have we fully taken on board your opinion?' Asking these questions with respect catapults the conversation and homes in on what may be wrong. The next step is to work through the options to address and rebalance any of the DRIVERS that are being quashed. If any one of the DRIVERS is undermined, the threat circuitry will be activated and performance and engagement depleted. If not dealt with, like skittles all the other DRIVERS will start to fall.

As leaders, for our teams we can affect the environment to support the DRIVERS. Leaders have between a 50%-70% impact on the culture of their team so your actions and decisions really matter. Using the DRIVERS, you can review your current approaches to performance management, communication, change and project management, and every daily interaction. Are the approaches brain-safe, engendering trust through supporting the DRIVERS? Is effort, learning and strengths rewarded? Is there a forced ranking system still in place that will undermine relative position? Does your flexible working strategy truly support autonomy and control or is it rule driven and in fact inflexible? Start to work with the DRIVERS little by little to build workplaces that support our reward circuitry. As each step is taken watch relationships deepen, engagement and wellbeing improve and performance grow. Work is a huge part of our world – let's make it a good part.

We are at the end of our journey. I have written this book to share with you what I have learnt through many years of experience and research because I firmly believe that we can make the world of work a better place. The next industrial age will bring as yet unknown and possibly unimaginable changes as artificial intelligence shifts our world. Deepening our understanding of each other and of ourselves allows us to bring back to the workplace what really unites us: humanity. Let's make work meaningful and value every single person's contribution and ideas. Let's build social capital through supporting inclusion, autonomy and choice. Let's ensure fairness and establish certainty where we can, and let us reward effort and provide space for real learning. Not so hard, is it? We have our five a day and our daily 30 minutes of exercise – why not add seven DRIVERS a day to the list? The rewards for our health, performance, economy and society will be far reaching. It is in our gift and is all our responsibility.

Good work and health.

Susanne

Notes

1 Paul Zak and Stephen Knack, 1998

2 Stephen Covey, *The Speed of Trust*

3 Trust, the key to building wellbeing and performance in the workplace, S. Jacobs 2013, Working Families

4 Dan Ariely, https://www.ted.com/talks/dan_ariely_what_makes_us_feel_good_about_our_work/transcript?language=en

5 Reference as preceding

6 *The Happiest People Pursue the Most Difficult Problems*, R. Moss Kanter, HBR April 10 2013 https://hbr.org/2013/04/to-find-happiness-at-work-tap.html

7 *Impact and the art of motivation maintenance: The effects of contact with beneficiaries on persistence behaviour*, Adam M. Grant, E.M. Campbell et al., Organisational Behaviour and Human Decision Processes, Vol. 103, Issue 1, 2007

8 *Patient Photos Spur Radiologist Empathy and Eye for Detail*, Dec 2008, RSNA http://www2.rsna.org/timssnet/media/pressreleases/pr_target.cfm?ID=389

9 *It's not all about me: motivating hand hygiene among health care professionals by focusing on patients*, Grant A.M., Hofman D.A., Psychol Sci. 2011 Dec, 22(12), pp 1494-9, epub Nov 10 2011

10 Ed Diener, Weiting Ng, James Harter, Raksha Arora, *Wealth and happiness across the world: Material prosperity predicts life evaluation, whereas psychosocial prosperity predicts positive feeling,* Journal of Personality and Social Psychology, 2010; *99 (1): 52 DOI: 10.1037/a0018066*

11 *Good to Great*, J. Collins, William Collins, 2001

12 GROW, Jim Stengel, Crown Business, NY http://www.jimstengel.com/ wp-content/uploads/2013/11/GrowChapterOne.pdf accessed 7 December 2017

13 *Built to Last: Successful Habits of Visionary Companies,* J. Collins & J.I. Porras, Random House Business Books, first published in 1994

14 *Corporate Culture and Performance,* J.P. Kotter & J.L. Heskett, The Free Press, 1992

15 Simon H. A., 1971, *Designing Organizations for an Information-Rich World*, in Martin Greenberger, Computers, Communication and the Public Interest, Baltimore, MD: The Johns Hopkins Press

16 Goleman D., *Focus: The Hidden Driver of Excellence*, 2013

17 *Purpose in Life and Its Relationship to All-Cause Mortality and Cardiovascular Events: A Meta-Analysis*; Cohen R., Bavishi C., Rozanski A., Psychosomatic Medicine: February/March 2016, Vol. 78, Issue 2, pp 122–133

18 *Subjective wellbeing, health, and ageing*, Prof Andrew Steptoe, Prof Angus Deaton, Prof Arthur A. Stone, The Lancet published online November 2014, Vol. 385, No. 9968, pp 640-648, 14 February 2015

19 *Sustained striatal activity predicts eudaemonic wellbeing and cortisol output*, Heller A.S., van Reekum C.M., Schaefer S.M., Lapate R.C., Radler B.T., Ryff C.D., Davidson R.J., Psychol Sci, 2013, Nov 1, 24(11), pp 2191-2200, epub Sep 20 2013

20 Blue Zones, Power 9, https://www.bluezones.com/2014/04/power-9/ accessed 12 July 2016

21 *Social Intelligence – the new science of human relationships*, D. Goleman, 2007, p 231

22 Tracy J.L. & Matsumoto D., 2008, *The spontaneous expression of pride and shame: evidence for biologically innate nonverbal displays*, Proceedings of the National Academy of Sciences of the United States of America, 105 (33), 11655-60 PMID: 18695237

23 *The Checklist Manifesto: How to get things right*, Atul Guwande, 2011

24 *Low-status compensation: A theory for understanding the role of status in cultures of honour*, Henry P.J., Journal of personality and social psychology, 2009, Vol. 9, No. 3, pp 451-466

25 *Somebodies and Nobodies*, Robert W. Fuller, 2003

26 *It's Good to be King, neurobiological benefits of higher social standing*, M. Akinola, W. Berry Mendes, Social Psychology & Personality Science, April 2013

27 *Status, Relative Pay, and Wage Growth, Evidence from M&A*, I. Kwon, E.M. Meyersson, Stanford Institute for Economic Policy Research, Stanford University, April 2007, SIEPR Discussion paper No. 07-26

28 Berger, Rosenholtz & Zelditch, 1980, Blau 1964

29 Baumeister & Leary 1995, Keltner, Gruenfield & Anderson, 2003

30 Haney C., Banks W.C. & Zimbardo P.G., 1973, *A study of prisoners and guards in a simulated prison,* Naval Research Review, 30, pp 4-17

31 Muir W. M., 2013, *Genetics and the Behaviour of Chickens: Welfare and Productivity,* In Genetics and the Behaviour of Domestic Animals, 2nd Edition, Vol. 2, pp 1-30

32 *Reading the Mind in the Eyes or Reading between the Lines? Theory of Mind Predicts Collective Intelligence Equally Well Online and Face-To-Face,* D. Engel, A. Williams, L.X Jing, C.F Chabris, T.W Malone, December 2014, PLOS http://dx.doi.org/10.1371/journal.pone.0115212 Accessed 4 August 2016

33 Baumeister R. & Leary M., 1995, *The need to belong: Desire for interpersonal attachments as a fundamental human motivation,* Psychological Bulletin, 117(3), pp 497-529

34 *Forget Survival of the Fittest: It Is Kindness That Counts,* Scientific America, February 2009, https://www.scientificamerican.com/article/kindness-emotions-psychology/ accessed 26 May 2015

35 *Born to Be Good: The Science of a Meaningful Life,* W.W. Norton, 2009, Dacher Keltner

36 DeWall C.N., MacDonald G., Webster G.D., Masten C.L., Baumeister R.F., Powell C., Eisenberger N.I., 2010, *Acetaminophen reduces social pain: Behavioural and neural evidence,* Psychological Science, 21 (7), pp 931–937

37 Masten C.L., Eisenberger N.I ., Pfeifer J.H. & Dapretto M., 2010, *Witnessing peer rejection during early adolescence: Neural correlates of empathy for experiences of social exclusion,* Social Neuroscience, 5 (5–6), pp 496–507

38 Abraham Maslow, *A Theory of Human Psychology,* Psychological Review, 1943

39 Perry B.D. & Pollard D., 1997, *Altered brain development following global neglect in early childhood,* Society For Neuroscience: Proceedings from Annual Meeting, New Orleans

40 *The Neurobiology of Human Relationships: Attachment and the Developing of the Social Brain,* L. Cozolino, 2014

41 Beauchaine T., *Vagal tone, development, and Gray's motivational theory: Toward an integrated model of autonomic nervous system functioning in psychopathology*, Development and Psychopathology, 2001,13, pp 183-214

42 Sober E., Wilson D.S., *Unto others: The evolution and psychology of unselfish behaviour*, Cambridge, MA: Harvard University Press

43 B.E. Kok, K.A. Coffey, M.A. Cohn, L.I. Catalino, T. Vacharkulksemsuk, S.B. Algoe, M. Brantley, B.L. Fredrickson, *How Positive Emotions Build Physical Health: Perceived Positive Social Connections Account for the Upward Spiral Between Positive Emotions and Vagal Tone*, Psychological Science, 2013

44 Blue Zones Project, *The Blue Zones – 9 lessons for living longer*, D. Buettner, 2004

45 Dunbar R.I.M., 1992, *Neocortex size as a constraint on group size in primates*, Journal of Human Evolution 22 (6), pp 469-493

46 *Care to Dare to Unleash Astonishing Employee Potential*, G. Kohlreiser, Insights IMD, No. 18, 2012

47 Reference as preceding

48 Reference as preceding

49 MacCoun R.J., 1996, *Sexual orientation and military cohesion: A critical review of the evidence*, In G. Herek, J. Jobe & R. Carney (eds.), Out in force: Sexual orientation and the military (pp 157-176). Chicago: University of Chicago Press

50 Lieberman M. D., 2013, *Social: Why Our Brains Are Wired To Connect*, Oxford University Press

51 Janis I.L., 1972, *Victims of Group-think*, New York: Houghton Mifflin

52 C. J. Nemeth, B. Personnaz, M. Personnaz, J.A. Goncalo, 2004, *The liberating role of conflict in group creativity: a study of two countries*, European Journal of Social Psychology, 34, pp 365-374

53 Ed. Catmull, *How Pixar fosters collective creativity*, HBR, September 2008, https://hbr.org/2008/09/how-pixar-fosters-collective-creativity

54 *Level and change in perceived control predict 19-year mortality: Findings from the Americans' changing lives study*; Infurna F. J., Ram N., Gerstorf D., Developmental Psychology, Vol. 49(10), Oct 2013, pp 1833-1847

55 *The effects of choice and enhanced personal responsibility for the aged: A field experiment in an institutional setting,* E.J. Langer & J. Rodin, Journal of Personality and Social Psychology 19, Vol. 34, No. 2, pp 191-198

56 *Seligman M.E.P., Maier S.F., 1967, Failure to escape traumatic shock,* Journal of Experimental Psychology 74 (1), pp 1-9; Overmier J.B., Seligman M.E.P., 1967, *Effects of inescapable shock upon subsequent escape and avoidance responding,* Journal of Comparative and Physiological Psychology 63 (1), pp 28-33

57 *Individual and mass behaviour in extreme situations,* Bettelheim B., The Journal of Abnormal and Social Psychology, Vol. 38(4), Oct 1943, pp 417-452. http://dx.doi.org/10.1037/h0061208

58 *Interactions between decision making and performance monitoring within prefrontal cortex,* Mark E. Walton, Joseph T. Devlin & Matthew F.S. Rushworth, *Nature Neuroscience 7,* pp 1259-1265 (2004) Published online 24 October 2004

59 *A Meta-Analysis of the Effectiveness of the 'But You Are Free' Compliance Gaining Technique,* DOI:10.1080/ 10510974.2012.727941, Christopher J. Carpenter, pp 6-17

60 Fincham F.D. & Rogge R., 2010, *Understanding Relationship Quality: Theoretical Challenges and New Tools for Assessment,* Journal of Family Theory and Review 2(4), pp 227-242; Hirshberger G., Srivastava S., Marsh P., Cowan C.P. & Cowan P.A., 2009, *Attachment, marital satisfaction, and divorce during the first fifteen years of parenthood,* Personal Relationships, 16, pp 401-420

61 Joseph G. Grzywacs, David M. Almeida & Daniel A. McDonald, 2002, *Work-Family Spillover and Daily Reports of Work and Family Stress in the Adult Labour Force,* Family Relations, 51, pp 28-36

62 D. Wheatley, *Autonomy in Paid Work and Employee Subjective Well-Being,* article first published online, 1 January 2017, https://doi.org/10.1177/0730888417697232

63 *Changing Work, Changing Health. Can Real Work-Time flexibility Promote Health Behaviours and Well-Being?* P. Moen, E.L. Kelly, E. Tranby, Q. Huang, Journal of Health and Social Behaviour, December 2011, Vol. 52, No. 4, pp 404-429

64 Peter, Laurence J., Hull, Raymond., 1969, *The Peter Principle: Why Things Always Go Wrong, p 8, New York*: William Morrow and Company

65 *Self-Regulation and the Problem of Human Autonomy: Does Psychology Need Choice, Self-Determination and Will?* R.M. Ryan & E.L. Deci, Journal of Personality, 74:6, December 2006

66 *The support of Autonomy and the Control of Behaviour,* E.L. Deci & R. M. Ryan, Journal of Personality and Social Psychology, 1987, Vol. 53, No. 6, pp 1022-1037

67 *Self-determination Theory Applied to Health Contexts: A Meta-Analysis;* Johan Y.Y., Nikos Ntoumanis, Cecilie Thøgersen-Ntoumani, Edward L. Deci, Richard M. Ryan, Joan L. Duda & Geoffrey C. Williams, Association for Psychological Science; Perspectives on Psychological Science7(4) pp 325-340

68 Reis H.T., Sheldon K.M., Gable S.L., Roscoe J. & Ryan R. M., 2000, *Daily well-being: The role of autonomy, competence, and relatedness,* Personality and Social Psychology Bulletin, 26, pp 419-435

69 La Guardia J. G., Ryan R. M., Couchman C. E. & Deci E. L., 2000, *Within person, variation in security of attachment: A self-determination theory perspective on attachment, need fulfilment, and wellbeing,* Journal of Personality and Social Psychology, 79, pp 367-384

70 Iyengar S. S. & Lepper M. R., 2000, *When choice is demotivating: Can one desire too much of a good thing?* Journal of Personality and Social Psychology, 79, pp 995-1006

71 *Perceived Self-Efficacy in Cognitive Development and Functioning,* 1993, A. Bandura, Educational Psychologist, 28(2), pp 117-148

72 Reference as preceding

73 Reference as preceding

74 *The Sunny Side of Fairness: Preference for Fairness Activates Reward Circuitry (and Disregarding Unfairness Activates Self-Control Circuitry)* Golnaz Tabibnia, Ajay B. Satpute & Matthew D. Lieberman, University of California, Los Angeles, Association for Psychological Science, Vol. 19, No. 4, pp 339-347

75 *Equity theory and fair inequality: a neuroeconomic study,* A.W. Cappelen et al., PNAS October 2014, Vol. 111, No. 43

76 Fehr E. & Schmidt K.M., 1999, *A theory of fairness, competition, and cooperation,* The Quarterly Journal of Economics 114 (3), pp 817-868

77 *CEOs Get Paid Too Much according to pretty much everyone in the world,* G Garrett, HBR 23/9/14 http://hbr.org/2014/09/CEOs-get-paid-too-much-accordinging-to-pretty-much-everyone-in-the-world/ Accessed 7 August 2015

78 *Building a better America – one wealth quintile at a time,* Michael L. Norton, Dan Ariely, Perspectives on Psychological Science 6 (1), pp 9-12, http://pps. Sage.pub. com/content/6/1/9 Accessed 7 August 2015

79 Gallup, April 2013, *1005 adults, gallup.com/poll/161927/majority-wealth-evenly-distribution.aspx.* Accessed 7 August 2015

80 *Towards an understanding of inequity,* J. Stacey Adams, The Journal of Abnormal and Social Psychology, Vol. 67(5), Nov 1963, pp 422-436, http://dx.doi. org/10.1037/h0040968

81 Adam Smith, *WN IV.Viii.30*

82 *http://www.caltech.edu/news/how-fairness-wired-brain-1423#sthash.w4rOmBMP. dpuf* Accessed 7 August 2015

83 *A two-year follow-up study of risk of depression according to work-unit measures of psychological demands and decision latitude,* Grynderup M.B, Mors O., Hansen Å.M., Andersen J.H., Bonde J.P., Kærgaard A., Kærlev L., Mikkelsen S., Rugulies R., Thomsen J.F., Kolstad H.A., Scand J., Work Environ Health, 2012 Nov, 38(6), pp 527-36. doi: 10.5271/sjweh.3316, epub 2012 Aug 10

84 Raihani N.J. & McAuliffe K., 2012, *Human punishment is motivated by inequity aversion, not a desire for reciprocity,* Biology Letters 8, pp 802-804

85 *Unfairness at work as a predictor of absenteeism,* E. M. De Boer, Arnold B. Baker, Jeff E. Syrott & Wilmar B. Shaufeli, Journal of Organisational Behaviour, J Organiz. Behav. 23, pp 181-197

86 *Intelligence,* Jeff Hawkins, 2004, Times Books

87 *Neural systems responding to degrees of uncertainty in human decision making,* M. Hsu, M. Bhatt, R. Adolphs, D. Tranel, C. Camerer, Science, Vol. 310, No. 5754, 9 December 2005, pp 1680-1683

88 *Midbrain dopamine neurons signal preference for advance information about upcoming rewards,* Ethan S. Bromberg-Martin, Okihide Hikosaka, National Institute of Health, Neuron 2009 July 16, 63 (1), pp 119-126 http://www.ncbi.nlm.nih.gov// pmc/articles/PMC2723053/pdf/nihms130281.pdf; Accessed 7 August 2015

89 *Hostage at the Table: How Leaders Can Overcome Conflict, Influence Others and Raise Performance,* G. Kohlrieser, Jossey-Bass, 2006

90 A. Furnham, J. Marks, *Tolerance of Ambiguity: A Review of the Recent Literature,* 2013, published online September 2013 in SciRes (http://www.scirp.org/journalpsych)

91 Frenkel-Brunswick E.,1949, *Tolerance toward ambiguity as a personality variable,* American Psychologist, 2, p 268

92 Caligiuri P.M., Jacobs R.R. & Farr J.L., 2000, *The attitudinal and behavioural openness scale: Scale development and construct validation,* International Journal of Intercultural Relations, 24, pp 27-46

93 Lauriola M., Levin I.P., & Hart S.S., 2007, *Common and distinct factors in decision making under ambiguity and risk: A psychometric study of individual differences,* Organisational Behaviour and Human Decision Process, 104, pp 130-149

94 Hofstede G. & Bond M.H., 1984, *Cultures and consequences,* Beverly Hills, C.A: Sage

95 Freeston M.H., Rheaume J.H., Duga M.J., & Ladouceur R., 1994, *Why do people worry?* Personality and individual Differences, 17, pp 791-802

96 The *Luck Factor: The Scientific Study of the Lucky Mind,* Richard Wiseman, Arrow Books

97 Wiseman R. *The Luck Factor: The Scientific Study of the Lucky Mind,* January 2004

98 *Breaking Bias,* Lierberman Matthew D., Rock David, Cox Christine L., Neuroleadership Journal, Vol. 5, May 2014

99 *Measuring Individual Differences in Implicit Cognition: The Implicit Association Test,* Greenwald A., McGhee D.E., Schwartz J.L.K., Journal of Personality and Social Psychology, 1998, Vol. 74, No. 6, pp 1464-1480

100 Damasio A., 1994, *Descartes Error: Reason, Emotion and the Human Brain*

101 *Leisure Time Spent Sitting in Relation to Total Mortality in a Prospective Cohort of US Adults,* A.V. Patel, L. Bernstein et al., American Journal of Epidemiology, April 2010

102 *Dominance Threat Display for Victory and Achievement in Competition Context,* D. Matsumoto & H. Hwang, Journal of Motivation, Emotion & Personality, January 2014

103 *Dominance, Politics and Physiology: Voters' Testosterone Changes on the Night of the 2008 United States Presidential Election,* S. Stanton et al., in PLoS ONE, 2009

104 Yerkes R.M., Dodson J.D., *The relation of strength of stimulus to rapidity of habit-formation,* J.Comp.Neurol.Psychol. 1908, 18, pp 459-482

105 Diamond D.M., *Cognitive, Endocrine and Mechanistic Perspectives on Non-Linear Relationships Between Arousal and Brain Function,* Nonlinearity in Biology, Toxicology, Medicine, 2005, 3(1), pp 1-7

106 The term Eustress was coined by endocrinologist Hans Seyle

107 Csikszentmihalyi, Mihaly, 1990, *Flow: The Psychology of Optimal Experience,* New York, NY: Harper and Row

108 *Perceived self-efficacy in Cognitive Development and Functioning,* A. Bandura, 1993, Educational Psychologist, 28(2), pp 117-148

109 *States of Curiosity Modulate Hippocampus-Dependent Learning via the Dopaminergic Circuit,* Gruber Matthias J. et al., Neuron, Vol. 84, Issue 2, pp 486-496

110 *Dopamine and Self-Directed Learning,* S. Herd, B. Mingus, R. O'Reilly, Department of Psychology and Neuroscience, University of Colorado, http://grey. colorado.edu/mediawiki/sites/mingus/images/c/c0/HerdMingusOReilly10.pdf; Accessed 30 October 2015

111 Martin et al., *Reducing Social Stress Elicits Emotional Contagion of Pain in Mouse and Human Strangers,* Current Biology (2015), published online Jan. 15, 2015, http://dx.doi.org/10.1016/j.cub.2014.11.028

About the Author

Susanne Jacobs

Susanne is a specialist in change, employee engagement, leadership and the science of optimal performance. Her work and research draws on over 25 years of strategic business change experience and commercial knowledge working across industry sectors, leading many major successful people and business change and restructuring programmes, both nationally and internationally.

Susanne completed her Masters in International Business with the business schools of Edinburgh University and Paris ENPC. She has postgraduate certificates in Organisational Development and Advanced Leadership Techniques and is a chartered fellow of the CIPD.

Susanne combines her in-depth senior leadership and business experience alongside the latest approaches from neuroscience and her own research to deliver practical, sustainable learning, tools and advice for leaders to improve performance, motivation and trust. Susanne's work has seen her named as one of the top thought leaders for trust.

Printed in Great Britain
by Amazon